Southern Living

The
SOUTHERN
HERITAGE
COOKBOOK
LIBRARY

The SOUTHERN HERITAGE
Breads
COOKBOOK

OXMOOR HOUSE
Birmingham, Alabama

Southern Living ®

The Southern Heritage Cookbook Library

Copyright 1983 by Oxmoor House, Inc.
Book Division of Southern Progress Corporation
P.O. Box 2463, Birmingham, Alabama 35201

Southern Living® is a federally registered trademark belonging to
Southern Living, Inc.

Library of Congress Catalog Number: 82-62139
ISBN:0-8487-0602-1

Manufactured in the United States of America

The Southern Heritage BREADS Cookbook

Manager, Editorial Projects: Ann H. Harvey
Southern Living® *Foods Editor*: Jean W. Liles
Production Editor: Joan E. Denman
Foods Editor: Katherine M. Eakin
Director, Test Kitchen: Laura N. Nestelroad
Test Kitchen Home Economists: Pattie B. Booker, Kay E. Clarke,
  Nancy Nevins, Elizabeth J. Taliaferro
Production Manager: Jerry R. Higdon
Copy Editor: Melinda E. West
Editorial Assistant: Karen P. Traccarella
Food Photographer: Jim Bathie
Food Stylist: Sara Jane Ball
Layout Designer: Christian von Rosenvinge
Mechanical Artist: Faith Nance
Research Assistant: Janice Randall

Special Consultants

Art Director: Irwin Glusker
Heritage Consultant: Meryle Evans
Foods Writer: Lillian B. Marshall
Food and Recipe Consultants: Marilyn Wyrick Ingram,
  Audrey P. Stehle

Cover (clockwise from back): Kentucky Sally Lynn (page 50), Ivy
Neck Light Bread (page 45), Biscuits with Sesame Seeds (page 83),
and Golden Corn Sticks (page 22). Photograph by George Ratkai.

A NICE SWHEAT GIRL.

CONTENTS

Clockwise from top: Skillet Cornbread (page 13), Basic White Bread (page 42), Old-Fashioned Cornbread (page 13), and Shirley Graham Muffins (page 110). Photographed in the original kitchen of Shirley Plantation.

INTRODUCTION

It has been pointed out by scholars that the bread and wine of the Lord's Supper is more than symbolic; it was the representative diet of the time, at least for those who could afford the wine. Egyptians, then Greeks, then Romans labored from sun to sun to earn two or three loaves of bread, their sole sustenance. Such continued to be the role of bread in the lives of the poor, even into "jolly" old England.

Early Europeans in this country brought with them this respect for the staff of life. Seeing the bounty of corn and the relative ease of its cultivation apparently convinced most of the newcomers that they need never starve. Indian corn was referred to as simply "Indian." In the North, settlers also grew some rye as well and were partial to a bread they called "rye 'n injun."

Good, but expensive, wheat flour was available in small quantities in the North by 1800. One Oliver Evans produced bolted flour in his watermill by a process patented in 1790. By the time Eliza Leslie got around to writing recipes, fine white flour was in fairly general use by well-to-do Northerners. The South imported flour from the North, as the German farmers in Texas were growing only enough for local use.

Ingredients other than good meal and flour were necessary to bring bread out of the staff-of-life, eat-it-or-starve category and elevate it to the forms we enjoy today. Leaven, anything that would make a lighter bread product, was actively pursued. Yeast, legacy from ancient Mesopotamia, was present, of course, and in the hands of experts it did produce a palatable result. Commercial yeast arrived in 1868. Well before that date, American inventiveness had manifested itself in the discovery of potash, a potassium carbonate leeched out of burned wood ash. Partially refined and called "pearlash," the new product did speed up baking most effectively, and the new republic of America was exporting 8,000 tons a year to England by 1792. The Holy Grail of quick leavening had been found. A footnote to that enterprise is that thousands of acres of forest were laid waste and burned for ashes.

Saleratus was another leavening agent available to cooks in the first half of the nineteenth century. Combined with an acid, it evolved into

The first specialty being good loaf bread, there was always a hot loaf for breakfast, hot corn bread for dinner, and a hot loaf for supper. Every house was famed for its loaf bread, and said a gentleman once to me: "Although at each place it is superb, yet each loaf differs from another loaf, preserving distinct characteristics which would enable me to distinguish, instantly, should there be a convention of loaves, the Oaklands loaf from the Greenfield loaf, and the Avenel loaf from the Rustic Lodge loaf."

Letitia M. Burwell
in "Letters from the Old Dominion"

baking powder in 1856: another plateau of progress. Passing decades brought vegetable shortenings and oils, self-rising flour, self-rising meal, biscuit and corn-bread mixes, pancake-waffle mix, and at last, the cake and icing mixes.

Developments such as these were concurrent with the changing American scene. Women working outside the home had less time to give to meal preparation and welcomed each new product. Home bakers began dwindling in numbers, too. At the turn of the century, they were buying ninety-five percent of the flour sold. By 1970, home bakers were accounting for only fifteen percent of that flour.

A more recent development has been the changing status of refined grains. White bread as the hallmark of luxury started centuries ago when only the rich could have it, and the poor man, trying to chew his stale crust of heavy whole-grain bread, was filled with envy. Since the early 1970s, public outcry at the bleaching agents and various additives in commercial bread has been heard by bakers. Darker, whole- or multi-grained breads are now to be had in great variety.

If the South had a coat of arms, it might consist of a corn pone rampant on a field, or roasting ears bordered by golden brown corn muffins. So accustomed are we to cornbread that it is one of the things we miss when, for any reason, we must remain abroad for any length of time. Not only Thomas Jefferson, but also Southern servicemen at war have grown homesick for the scratchy nourishment of their childhood. We still enjoy hoecakes but find no dinner table too lavish to accommodate a fine dish of spoonbread.

Nostalgia plays a part in our devotion to the old self-starters: salt-rising and sourdough breads. The challenge is there, admittedly. But the end result, once patience has won out, is one of the most rewarding of kitchen adventures. In the main, bear in mind that warmth, unremitting warmth, is needed and *time*. A compromise with any self-starter is to add a little commercial yeast to speed things along.

When a cook says, "I haven't the time to bake with yeast," perhaps this hint will help: The primary fermentation (first rising) of any yeast dough can take place in the refrigerator overnight. Retarded by the cold, the dough will slowly double in bulk and be ready in the morning for shaping, another rising, and baking. You'll find, as you read on, that rye flour must have unbleached (or all-purpose) or bread flour added to it because it has not enough gluten to react with yeast. And, also, that rye dough is somewhat sticky by nature. Mainly, yeast baking is a time to relax; yeast works hard enough for both of you.

If a quicker bread is desired, muffins may be just the thing. Choose one made famous by The Peabody Hotel in Memphis or the one they make with rice in Charleston, and it will be "Hail to the chef!"

To offer a Southerner his choice between cornbread and biscuits is to torture him unnecessarily. The honorable thing to do is offer both. Fine biscuits have been the signature of Southern cooking since before anyone can remember. The lesson here is that biscuit dough, unlike yeast breads that must be kneaded, cannot take handling. The dough should err on the soft side. If a food processor is used at all, mix the dry ingredients with it, work in the shortening, and then remove the contents to a mixing bowl before stirring the liquid. The processor can overwork biscuit dough in two seconds flat.

Many experienced bakers use a canvas or heavy cloth with flour liberally rubbed into it for bread and pastry work. The hands need not touch the soft biscuit dough, as corner after corner is brought over, folding the dough. Usually just a few such folds will smooth the dough for cutting. This method prevents overhandling and working in too much flour, as is sometimes done on a hard work surface. Biscuits, once mastered, lend themselves to countless applications, from cheese-flavored party savories to teatime sweets.

It only takes one visit to New Orleans' French Market to catch "beignet fever." Burning hot from frying oil and sinfully sugared, beignets can be instantly addictive. One may allay the craving by (1) moving to New Orleans or (2) learning to make them. Doughnuts, yeast and otherwise, are here, along with Arkansas corn flapjacks and tortillas out of the Southwest.

Here, too, are the most special baked things from our chequered heritage: scones, crumpets, Graham crackers, apple strudel, French breakfast puffs . . . you may even make your own soda crackers. Have a care, though; a Rebel yell is hiding between these covers.

CORN! CORN! CORN!

American Indians had been cultivating corn for over two thousand years by the time the Europeans arrived. This meant that corn could no longer re-seed itself; it had to be farmed. And its cultivation was a life-saving lesson the Indians taught the newcomers.

The first cornbread was a wonder of simplicity, probably not what we would consider appetizing. But it was a nourishing whole-grain bread. Ash cakes were made by forming the dough by hand, then dropping the lumps directly into hot ashes. When cooked, the bread was dusted off and eaten, all the better for the residual ash flavor. Johnny cake, doubtless named for the durable, packable "journey cake," was closely related to the other early cornbreads such as sad bread, water cake, flat cake, hoecake, and corn dodgers. They were uniformly hard and dry.

Iron utensils such as the "spider," a three-legged skillet with a concave lid for holding hot coals for even baking, the griddle, and the skillet helped improve the quality of cornbread. The cook could add more liquid to the mixture without risking the batter flowing off the hoe or out into the ashes.

Slowly but surely, the palatability of cornbread was improved by the addition of eggs, milk, and, in the 1800s, baking powder. Soon after, Southerners discovered that cracklings, a by-product of lard-making, made a delicious additive, while in the Southwest settlers superheated their cornbread with jalapēno peppers.

The importance of corn in Southern economics cannot be over-emphasized: Leftover cornbread was eaten with milk or hot gravy. "Secondary consumption" has always had a crucial place in our meat production: Corn sileage for cattle, mash for chickens, green or dried corn for fattening shoats. From the suckers (corms) pulled and eaten like asparagus, to the last dust of meal, corn has continued to nourish the Southerner and his livestock to this day. And that does not even count all the corn it takes to keep us in our favorite beverage.

Here is cornbread, from staple to ultimate refinement: souffléed spoonbread.

Alabama Cornsticks (front), Mrs. Paul's Cornmeal Cakes (left), and Cassie's Egg Cornbread photographed at McCalla, Alabama. Overshot waterwheel mill, part of Tannehill Historic State Park, was built in 1838 by John Wesley Hall and is in working order.

OLD-FASHIONED CORNBREAD

4 cups cornmeal
2 teaspoons baking soda
2 teaspoons salt
4 eggs, beaten
4 cups buttermilk
½ cup bacon drippings

Combine dry ingredients; add eggs and buttermilk, mixing well. Stir in bacon drippings.

Heat a well-greased 10½-inch cast-iron skillet in a 400° oven for 3 minutes or until very hot. Pour batter into hot skillet. Bake at 450° for 40 minutes or until golden brown. Yield: 8 to 10 servings.

DEEP SOUTH CORNBREAD

1½ cups cornmeal
½ cup all-purpose flour
1 tablespoon baking powder
1 teaspoon salt
1½ cups milk
¼ cup vegetable oil

Combine cornmeal, flour, baking powder, and salt; mix well. Stir in milk just until dry ingredients are moistened. Add oil to batter, stirring well.

Heat a well-greased 8-inch cast-iron skillet in a 400° oven for 3 minutes or until very hot. Pour batter into hot skillet. Bake at 425° for 30 minutes or until lightly browned. Yield: 6 servings.

Up-dated Johnny Cake in company with cornhusk dolls.

SKILLET CORNBREAD

2 cups cornmeal
2 teaspoons baking powder
½ teaspoon baking soda
2 teaspoons salt
4 eggs, beaten
1½ cups buttermilk
1 cup water
1 tablespoon shortening

Sift together dry ingredients. Combine eggs, buttermilk, and water; slowly stir into cornmeal mixture just until dry ingredients are moistened.

Melt shortening in a 9-inch cast-iron skillet in a 400° oven for 3 minutes or until very hot. Pour batter into hot skillet. Bake at 425° for 35 minutes or until lightly browned. Yield: 6 to 8 servings.

JOHNNY CAKE

¾ cup all-purpose flour
1 teaspoon baking soda
2 tablespoons sugar
½ teaspoon salt
1¼ cups cornmeal
2 eggs, beaten
¼ cup vinegar
¼ cup shortening, melted

Sift together flour, soda, sugar, and salt; stir in cornmeal. Combine eggs, vinegar, and shortening; add to dry ingredients, stirring just until moistened.

Heat a well-greased 9-inch cast-iron skillet in a 400° oven for 3 minutes. Spoon batter into hot skillet. Bake at 400° for 30 minutes or until lightly browned. Yield: 8 servings.

CASSIE'S EGG CORNBREAD

Cassie was a cook serving the residents of Tolville, Arkansas, from the late 1920s through the 1940s. Her Egg Cornbread was a favorite.

½ teaspoon baking soda
2 cups buttermilk
2 cups cornmeal
1 teaspoon baking powder
1 tablespoon sugar
2 eggs, beaten

Dissolve soda in buttermilk; stir well. Combine cornmeal, baking powder, and sugar. Add eggs and buttermilk mixture, mixing well.

Heat a well-greased 9-inch cast-iron skillet in a 400° oven for 3 minutes or until very hot. Pour batter into hot skillet. Bake at 425° for 30 minutes or until lightly browned. Yield: 6 to 8 servings.

JOHNS ISLAND CORNBREAD

1 cup lard
¼ cup sugar
2 eggs, beaten
1¾ cups cornmeal
1¼ cups all-purpose flour
2 tablespoons baking powder
1 teaspoon salt
1¼ cups milk

Combine lard and sugar, beating well. Add eggs; beat well. Sift together cornmeal, flour, baking powder, and salt. Add to creamed mixture alternately with milk, beginning and ending with flour mixture.

Spoon batter into a greased 13- x 9- x 2-inch baking pan. Bake at 450° for 25 minutes or until golden brown. Yield: 15 to 18 servings.

OKLAHOMA CRACKLING CORNBREAD

1¾ cups cornmeal
¼ cup all-purpose flour
1 teaspoon baking powder
1 teaspoon baking soda
2 eggs, beaten
2 cups buttermilk
1 cup cracklings

Combine cornmeal, flour, baking powder, and soda; mix well. Add eggs, buttermilk, and cracklings, stirring well.

Heat a well-greased 9-inch cast-iron skillet in a 400° oven for 3 minutes. Pour batter into hot skillet. Bake at 400° for 35 minutes or until golden brown. Yield: 6 to 8 servings.

A George Catlin sketch of Green Corn Dance or "Busk," chief ceremony of the Creeks of Georgia and Alabama.

The New-York Historical Society

Oklahoma Crackling Bread is an addition to any meal.

CORNBREAD WITH CORN

1 cup self-rising cornmeal
½ cup butter or margarine, melted
2 eggs, beaten
1 cup cream-style corn
1 cup commercial sour cream
2 tablespoons grated onion

Combine all ingredients, mixing well.

Heat a well-greased 9-inch cast-iron skillet in a 400° oven for 3 minutes or until very hot. Pour batter into hot skillet. Bake at 400° for 40 minutes or until golden brown. Cool 10 minutes. Cut cornbread into wedges to serve. Yield: 6 to 8 servings.

FRESH CORN BREAD

5 ears fresh corn
3 eggs, beaten
¾ cup milk
¼ cup plus 1½ teaspoons bacon drippings
1½ tablespoons sugar
1 tablespoon baking powder
¾ teaspoon salt
½ cup plus 1 tablespoon all-purpose flour

Cut corn from cob, scraping cob to remove the pulp. Combine corn, eggs, milk, bacon drippings, sugar, baking powder, and salt; stir well. Gradually stir in flour.

Heat a well-greased 8-inch cast-iron skillet in a 400° oven for 3 minutes or until very hot. Pour batter into hot skillet, and bake at 425° for 25 minutes or until golden brown. Yield: 6 servings.

MOCK CRACKLING BREAD

1 cup yellow cornmeal
1 cup all-purpose flour
1 tablespoon plus 1 teaspoon baking powder
1 tablespoon sugar
½ teaspoon salt
1½ cups milk
¼ cup shortening, melted
1 egg, beaten
10 slices bacon, cooked and crumbled
Creole Celery Sauce

Combine cornmeal, flour, baking powder, sugar, and salt; add milk, shortening, and egg, mixing well. Stir in bacon.

Pour batter into a well-greased 8-inch square pan. Bake at 425° for 25 minutes or until lightly browned. Cut into squares, and serve with Creole Celery Sauce. Yield: 9 servings.

Creole Celery Sauce:

1 medium-size green pepper, chopped
⅓ cup grated carrot
1 tablespoon minced onion
3 tablespoons bacon drippings
2 tablespoons all-purpose flour
¾ cup chicken broth
½ cup tomato soup, undiluted
1 cup chopped celery
½ teaspoon salt
¼ teaspoon black pepper
⅛ teaspoon red pepper

Sauté green pepper, carrot, and onion in bacon drippings until tender; add flour, stirring until smooth. Cook 1 minute, stirring constantly. Gradually add broth and tomato soup; cook over medium heat, stirring constantly, until thickened and bubbly. Stir in remaining ingredients. Yield: 2 cups.

Choose Jalapeño Cornbread (top), Special Cornbread (right), or Ranch Cornbread.

RANCH CORNBREAD

1 cup cornmeal
1 cup all-purpose flour
1 tablespoon plus 1 teaspoon
  baking powder
2 tablespoons sugar
1 teaspoon salt
1½ cups milk
2 eggs, beaten
½ cup diced cooked ham
½ cup (2 ounces) shredded
  sharp Cheddar cheese
½ cup chopped green pepper
¼ cup chopped pimiento

Combine dry ingredients; add milk and eggs, mixing well. Stir in remaining ingredients.

Heat a well-greased 9-inch cast-iron skillet in a 400° oven for 3 minutes. Pour batter into hot skillet. Bake at 425° for 30 minutes or until golden brown. Yield: 6 to 8 servings.

JALAPEÑO CORNBREAD

1 cup cornmeal
1 cup all-purpose flour
1 tablespoon baking
  powder
¾ teaspoon salt
2 eggs, slightly beaten
1 cup milk
2 tablespoons bacon
  drippings
1 cup whole kernel corn
1 large jalapeño pepper,
  chopped
3 tablespoons chopped
  pimiento

Combine all ingredients; mixing well. Pour batter into a greased 8-inch square pan. Bake at 350° for 35 minutes or until lightly browned. Yield: 9 servings.

SPECIAL CORNBREAD

1 cup cornmeal
¼ cup all-purpose flour
2 teaspoons baking powder
¼ teaspoon baking soda
1 teaspoon sugar
1 teaspoon salt
1 (14½-ounce) can whole
  tomatoes, undrained and
  chopped
1 medium onion, chopped
1 egg, beaten
3 tablespoons shortening,
  melted

Combine dry ingredients; add tomatoes, onion, egg, and shortening, mixing well.

Heat a well-greased 9-inch cast-iron skillet in a 400° oven for 3 minutes or until very hot. Pour batter into hot skillet. Bake at 400° for 30 minutes. Yield: 6 to 8 servings.

CORN LIGHT BREAD

2 cups cornmeal
1 cup all-purpose flour
1 teaspoon baking powder
½ cup sugar
1 teaspoon salt
1 teaspoon baking soda
2 cups buttermilk
⅓ cup water
3 tablespoons bacon
    drippings

Combine cornmeal, flour, baking powder, sugar, and salt, mixing well. Dissolve soda in buttermilk; add to cornmeal mixture, stirring well. Add remaining ingredients; mix well.

Spoon batter into a well-greased 8½- x 4½- x 3-inch loaf pan. Bake at 350° for 1 hour or until golden brown. Yield: 1 loaf.

CORNMEAL SALLY LUNN

2 cups cornmeal
1 teaspoon baking soda
½ teaspoon salt
1¼ cups buttermilk
1 (8-ounce) carton
    commercial sour cream

Combine cornmeal, baking soda, and ½ teaspoon salt; add buttermilk and sour cream, mixing well. Pour batter into a well-greased 9-inch pieplate. Bake at 350° for 40 minutes or until lightly browned. Yield: 6 to 8 servings.

"Take the trouble to get meal water-ground, from white flint corn, and fresh from the mill. Then you will have something worth spending time and effort upon—spending them hopefully. Why, the wisest man can not tell—but steam-ground meal is of a flavor wholly unlike that of water-ground."

Dishes & Beverages of the Old South, 1913.

Valentine Museum, Richmond, Virginia

17

LITTLE CORN TREATS

TENNESSEE CORNMEAL MUFFINS

1½ cups cornmeal
1 teaspoon baking soda
1 teaspoon sugar
1 teaspoon salt
2 eggs, beaten
2 cups buttermilk
3 tablespoons lard, melted

Combine cornmeal, soda, sugar, and salt. Combine remaining ingredients; add to dry ingredients, mixing well.

Heat well-greased muffin pans in a 400° oven for 3 minutes or until very hot. Spoon batter into hot muffin pans, filling three-fourths full. Bake at 400° for 25 minutes or until lightly browned. Yield: 1½ dozen.

SAUSAGE CORN MUFFINS

2 cups all-purpose flour
¾ cup cornmeal
2 teaspoons baking powder
2 tablespoons sugar
½ teaspoon salt
1¾ cups milk
1 egg, beaten
½ pound bulk pork sausage

Combine flour, cornmeal, baking powder, sugar, and salt; mix well. Stir in milk and egg just until dry ingredients are moistened. Stir in sausage.

Spoon batter into greased muffin pans, filling two-thirds full. Bake at 425° for 25 minutes or until golden brown. Yield: about 1½ dozen.

CRACKLING CORNBREAD MUFFINS

2 cups cornmeal
½ cup all-purpose flour
1 tablespoon baking powder
2 teaspoons salt
1 egg, beaten
2 cups milk
1 cup cracklings

Combine cornmeal, flour, baking powder, and salt; stir in egg and milk. Add cracklings to batter, stirring well.

Heat two well-greased muffin pans in a 400° oven for 3 minutes or until very hot. Pour batter into hot muffin pans, filling two-thirds full. Bake at 350° for 30 minutes or until golden brown. Yield: about 2 dozen.

1909: This Virginian took the prize and posed with his corn.

Valentine Museum, Richmond, Virginia

For every object once useful but now neglected, there is a collector. Apple corers, butter molds, trivets, crimping irons...the list is long. Old muffin irons and stick pans, some stamped "Griswold," some "Wagner," and some not even identified by the manufacturer, are now a highly collectible part of Americana. Some of the ornate, shallow "muffin" irons were used to form cakes of maple sugar. Muffins and sticks baked in them are most attractive to serve, with more crust per bite and usually quite tender, as their batters tend to be thinner. The iron is always preheated in the oven before the batter is baked.

The utensils at the right are from a private collection in Alabama of over 700 muffin and cornstick pans.

Marion Harland, 1831 - 1922

By the time she was in her late twenties, Virginia-born Marion Harland's name had become a household word. But her real name, Mary Virginia Hawes Terhune, never was. Most of the readers of her many novels, her *Complete Cookbook,* and *Common Sense in the Household* did not know that she was the wife of one of the foremost clerics of the day, Edward Payson Terhune.

When she published her autobiography in 1910 at the age of seventy-nine, Marion Harland's name was known all over America. Of her decision to tell the *Story of My Long Life,* she wrote, "The idea of reviewing that life upon paper first came to me with the consciousness which was almost a shock — that, of all the authors still on active professional duty in our country, I am the only one whose memory runs back to the state of national history that preceded the Civil War by a quarter-century. I, alone, am left to tell, of my own knowledge and experience, what the old South was in deed and in truth...."

MARION HARLAND'S CORN DODGERS

1 cup cornmeal
1 cup boiling water
2 tablespoons bacon
 drippings
½ teaspoon salt

Combine all ingredients, mixing well. Mound batter by tablespoonfuls onto a lightly greased baking sheet. Bake at 400° for 30 minutes. Yield: 1 dozen.

NORTH CAROLINA CORNMEAL CRISPS

1 cup cornmeal
1¼ cups boiling water
2 tablespoons lard, melted
½ teaspoon salt

Combine all ingredients, mixing well. Spoon batter by tablespoonfuls onto a lightly greased baking sheet. Bake at 400° for 20 minutes or until edges are browned. Yield: about 1½ dozen.

Marion Harland's Corn Dodgers: A Virginia heritage.

SCRATCH BACKS

3 cups boiling water
3 cups cornmeal
1 teaspoon bacon drippings
1 teaspoon salt

Pour water slowly over cornmeal in a large mixing bowl, stirring well. Stir in bacon drippings and salt.

Drop batter by 2 tablespoonfuls onto lightly greased baking sheets. (Stir mixture frequently to prevent cornmeal from settling.) Bake at 400° for 25 minutes or until lightly browned. Yield: about 3 dozen.

CORNMEAL BISCUITS

1½ cups all-purpose flour
½ cup yellow cornmeal
2½ teaspoons baking powder
½ teaspoon salt
⅓ cup shortening
¾ cup milk

Combine flour, cornmeal, baking powder, and salt; stir well. Cut in shortening with a pastry blender until mixture resembles coarse meal. Sprinkle milk evenly over flour mixture, stirring just until dry ingredients are moistened.

Turn dough out onto a lightly floured surface, and knead 10 to 12 times.

Roll dough to ½-inch thickness; cut with a 2-inch biscuit cutter. Place biscuits on greased baking sheets. Bake at 450° for 10 minutes or until biscuits are lightly browned. Yield: about 2 dozen.

GOLDEN CORN STICKS

1½ cups cornmeal
¼ cup all-purpose flour
2 teaspoons baking powder
¼ teaspoon baking soda
1 teaspoon salt
1 cup buttermilk
2 eggs, beaten
2 tablespoons shortening, melted

Combine cornmeal, flour, baking powder, soda, and salt; mix well. Add buttermilk and eggs, stirring just until dry ingredients are moistened. Stir shortening into batter.

Heat well-greased cast-iron corn stick pans in a 400° oven for 3 minutes or until very hot. Spoon batter into pans, filling two-thirds full. Bake at 400° for 25 minutes or until lightly browned. Yield: 14 corn sticks.

ALABAMA CORN STICKS

1½ cups cornmeal
1½ teaspoons baking powder
¾ teaspoon baking soda
½ teaspoon sugar
½ teaspoon salt
1½ cups buttermilk
1 egg, beaten

Sift together cornmeal, baking powder, soda, sugar, and salt; stir in buttermilk and egg, mixing well.

Heat well-greased cast-iron corn stick pans in a 400° oven for 3 minutes or until very hot. Spoon batter into pans, filling two-thirds full. Bake at 400° for 25 minutes or until lightly browned. Yield: 14 corn sticks.

Cornshucking at Uncle Henry Garrett's Tallyho Farm near Stem, North Carolina, 1939.

University of North Carolina, Chapel Hill

OKLAHOMA CORNMEAL ROLLS

1½ cups all-purpose flour
¾ cup cornmeal
1 tablespoon baking powder
¼ teaspoon baking soda
1 teaspoon sugar
1 teaspoon salt
2 tablespoons shortening
1 egg, beaten
1 cup buttermilk

Sift together dry ingredients. Cut in shortening until mixture resembles coarse meal. Add egg and buttermilk, stirring just until dry ingredients are moistened. Turn dough out onto a lightly floured surface; knead lightly 3 or 4 times.

Roll dough to ¼-inch thickness; cut into 2½-inch circles. Make a crease across each circle, and fold one half over. Gently press edges to seal.

Place on a greased baking sheet. Bake at 450° for 15 minutes or until lightly browned. Yield: about 1½ dozen.

CHEROKEE CORN PONES

2 cups cornmeal
¼ teaspoon baking soda
1 teaspoon salt
½ cup shortening
¾ cup buttermilk
¾ cup milk
Butter or margarine

Combine cornmeal, baking soda, and salt; cut in shortening until mixture resembles coarse meal. Add buttermilk and milk, stirring just until dry ingredients are moistened.

Form batter into eight ½-inch thick cakes. Place on a hot greased griddle. Bake at 400° for 15 minutes. Turn and bake an additional 15 minutes. Serve hot with butter. Yield: 8 pones.

Virginia Corn Pones, Golden Corn Sticks, and Oklahoma Cornmeal Rolls in front of grindstone at Hall's Mill.

VIRGINIA CORN PONES

3 cups cornmeal
1 teaspoon baking powder
½ teaspoon baking soda
1 teaspoon sugar
1 teaspoon salt
3 tablespoons shortening, melted
1 cup plus 2 tablespoons buttermilk
1 cup plus 2 tablespoons water

Combine dry ingredients; mix well. Add shortening, buttermilk, and water; stir just until dry ingredients are moistened.

Shape into oblong patties, using ⅓ cup batter per patty. (Stir mixture frequently to prevent cornmeal from settling.) Place on lightly greased baking sheets. Bake at 450° for 10 minutes or until lightly browned. Yield: about 1½ dozen.

KENTUCKY CORN PONES

1 cup cornmeal
½ teaspoon salt
½ cup boiling water
½ cup plus 1 tablespoon
  whipping cream
1 tablespoon butter or
  margarine, melted
1 teaspoon baking powder

Combine cornmeal and salt; add boiling water, and stir well. Add remaining ingredients, mixing well.

Drop mixture by tablespoonfuls onto a greased griddle. Bake at 450° for 15 minutes or until edges are lightly browned. Yield: 6 servings.

TENNESSEE CRACKLING PONES

3 cups water
1 cup cracklings
1½ cups cornmeal
1 teaspoon salt

Bring water to a boil; reduce heat, and add cracklings. Cook over medium heat 5 minutes or until cracklings are tender. Remove from heat, and add cornmeal and salt. Stir well.

Shape into patties, using ½ cup batter for each patty. Place patties on a well-greased baking sheet or griddle. Bake at 450° for 45 minutes or until pones are lightly browned. Yield: 6 servings.

SWEET POTATO CORN PONES

1 teaspoon baking soda
1¼ cups buttermilk
2 cups cornmeal
1 tablespoon sugar
1 teaspoon salt
1 cup cooked, mashed sweet
  potatoes
1 egg, beaten
2 tablespoons bacon
  drippings

Dissolve soda in buttermilk; stir well. Combine cornmeal, sugar, and salt; add buttermilk mixture, sweet potato, egg, and drippings, mixing well.

Shape into balls, using 1 tablespoon batter per ball. Place on greased griddle, and lightly press into circles with the back of a fork. Bake at 400° for 20 minutes. Yield: about 3 dozen.

Nineteenth-century advertisement for cornmeal, staff of life.

Some food historians trace the origin of the word pone to the Algonquian word *apan*, which meant baked. In its primitive form, pone furnished Indian and settler alike with nourishing, high-fiber food even when game and fresh vegetation were scarce. Coarse-ground corn and water were the rock-bottom ingredients and, although there were no recipes for it, creative cooks often added dried berries or honey for a pleasant change in flavor.

Both the taste and the texture bore little resemblance to cornbread as we know it. Forming the pones must have been similar to handling wet sand. Sometimes the pone was boiled, which may have been tastier, especially if cooked with meat or vegetables as are the cornmeal dumplings Southerners still make today.

FLAPJACKS AND HUSH PUPPIES

Syrupy smiles go with pancakes in this 1930s movie "still."

CORNMEAL BATTY CAKES

1 cup cornmeal
½ teaspoon baking soda
½ teaspoon salt
1 egg, beaten
1¼ cups buttermilk

Sift together dry ingredients; add egg and buttermilk, stirring until smooth.

Drop batter by tablespoonfuls onto a hot, lightly greased griddle. Turn cakes when tops are covered with bubbles and edges are browned. Drain well on paper towels, and serve hot. Yield: 20 small cakes.

MRS. PAUL'S CORNMEAL CAKES

1 egg, well beaten
¾ cup buttermilk
1 cup cornmeal
2 tablespoons all-purpose flour
2 teaspoons baking powder
¼ teaspoon salt
1 tablespoon shortening, melted
Butter or margarine

Combine egg and buttermilk, mixing well. Combine dry ingredients; stir into egg mixture. Stir in shortening.

Drop batter by 2 tablespoonfuls onto a hot, lightly greased griddle or skillet. (Stir mixture frequently to prevent cornmeal from settling.) Turn cakes when tops are covered with bubbles and edges are browned. Serve hot with butter. Yield: 1 dozen.

Arkansas Cornmeal Flapjacks, prelude to a cheerful, busy day.

ALABAMA CORN GRIDDLE CAKES

½ cup cornmeal
1½ cups boiling water
1 cup milk
2¼ cups all-purpose flour
1 tablespoon baking powder
⅓ cup sugar
1½ teaspoons salt
1 egg, beaten
2 tablespoons butter or
  margarine, melted
Butter or margarine

Combine cornmeal and water in a large mixing bowl; stir well. Set aside for 5 minutes.

Gradually add milk to cornmeal mixture, stirring well. Sift together flour, baking powder, sugar, and salt; stir into cornmeal mixture. Add beaten egg and 2 tablespoons melted butter; stir well.

Drop batter by 2 tablespoonfuls onto a hot, lightly greased griddle. (Stir mixture frequently to prevent cornmeal from settling.) Turn cakes when tops are covered with bubbles and edges are browned. Serve hot with butter. Yield: about 2 dozen.

KENTUCKY LACE CAKES

1½ cups cornmeal
1 teaspoon baking
  powder
1 teaspoon baking soda
1 teaspoon salt
2 eggs, beaten
2 tablespoons bacon
  drippings
2 cups buttermilk

Combine all ingredients, and mix well. Drop batter by 2 tablespoonfuls onto a hot, lightly greased griddle. Turn cakes when tops are bubbly and edges are browned. Serve immediately. Yield: about 3 dozen.

ARKANSAS CORNMEAL FLAPJACKS

1 teaspoon baking soda
2 cups buttermilk
1½ cups cornmeal
½ cup all-purpose flour
2 teaspoons sugar
½ teaspoon salt
2 eggs, beaten
2 tablespoons vegetable oil
Butter or margarine
  (optional)
Maple syrup or sorghum
  (optional)

Dissolve soda in buttermilk; stir well. Combine dry ingredients; add eggs and buttermilk mixture, mixing well. Add oil, mixing lightly.

Pour ¼ cup batter onto a hot, lightly greased griddle or skillet. Turn flapjacks when tops are covered with bubbles and edges are browned. Serve hot with butter and syrup, if desired. Yield: 1½ dozen.

INDIAN HOECAKES

1 cup cornmeal
1 cup milk, scalded
½ teaspoon salt
1 tablespoon lard, melted
Butter or margarine

Combine cornmeal and milk; mix well. Add salt and lard, and stir well.

Drop batter by 2 tablespoonfuls onto a hot, lightly greased griddle. Turn cakes when tops are bubbly and edges are browned. Serve hot with butter. Yield: 1 dozen.

Handwritten and illustrated recipe, 1852.

HOT WATER HOECAKES

2 cups cornmeal
3 cups boiling water
2 tablespoons shortening
1 teaspoon salt
1 egg, beaten
About ½ cup milk
Butter

Stir cornmeal slowly into boiling water in a saucepan. Add shortening, salt, egg, and enough milk to make a stiff batter. Shape into small ½-inch-thick cakes. Fry on a hot greased griddle until golden brown, turning once. Serve hot with butter. Yield: about 20.

Traditionally, cornbread recipes were passed down in the vaguest of terms as in this captivating recipe for snow cakes from an 1893 cookbook: "Take one part Indian meal and two parts of dry snow; mix well in a cold room. Fill the pans rounding full, and bake immediately in a very hot oven."

For cooks in the far South where snow is scarce, here are more useful recipes.

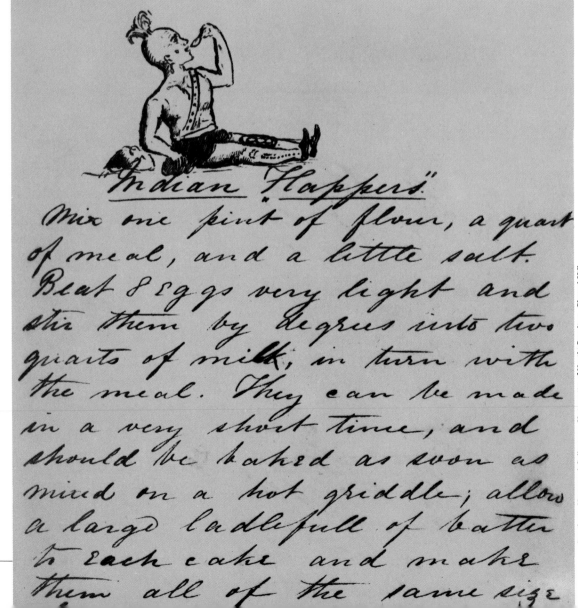

"Indian Flappers"

Mix one pint of flour, a quart of meal, and a little salt. Beat 8 eggs very light and stir them by degrees into two quarts of milk; in turn with the meal. They can be made in a very short time; and should be baked as soon as mixed on a hot griddle; allow a large ladlefull of batter to each cake and make them all of the same size

Camp dinner along the Little Miami River in Florida, c.1900.

CROSS CREEK HUSH PUPPIES

1 cup cornmeal
2 teaspoons baking
  powder
½ teaspoon salt
1 medium onion, finely
  chopped
1 egg, slightly beaten
⅓ cup milk
Vegetable oil

Combine cornmeal, baking powder, and salt; stir well. Add chopped onion and egg, mixing well. Slowly add milk, stirring just until dry ingredients are moistened.

Carefully drop batter by tablespoonfuls into deep, hot oil (375°), cooking only a few at a time. Fry about 2 minutes; turn and fry an additional 2 minutes or until hush puppies are golden brown. Drain well on paper towels. Yield: 1 dozen.

It would be hard to find a Southern dish that admits of as many interpretations and backgrounds as does the hush puppy. Having no sworn testimony as to the naming of the tasty little thing, we are free to choose among several explanations. We are informed on good authority that the hush puppy came from Georgia. Or Mississippi. Certainly Marjorie Kinnan Rawlings put it in the Southern lexicon in *Cross Creek Cookery.*

The theory that the term started as a mixture of hash and batter called "hash puppy" has few adherents. Others say some fishermen were sitting by their campfire after dining on fried fish when their huntin' dawgs started to whine. The men fried some cornbread batter in the skillet they had used for frying the fish and tossed it to the dogs.

"Hush, puppies," the men said. They were nice men. Did they put chopped onion in the batter? History, even gossip, is silent on that point.

Some of us grew up eating hush puppies (deep-fried, not skillet-fried) as a side dish with fish. Those hush puppies always contained onion; the famous Stagecoach Inn at Salado, Texas, does not use onion. What *is* the straight story?

An assortment of hush puppies.

The Stagecoach Inn at Salado, Texas.

STAGECOACH INN HUSH PUPPIES

3½ cups water
2 cups cornmeal
1 teaspoon baking powder
3 tablespoons sugar
1½ teaspoons salt
¼ cup butter or margarine, softened
Vegetable oil

Bring water to a boil in a small Dutch oven. Combine cornmeal, baking powder, sugar, and salt; slowly add to boiling water, stirring constantly until mixture is smooth. Remove from heat; add butter, stirring until melted. Cool mixture 10 minutes.

Shape batter into 3- x 1-inch oblong rolls. Deep fry in hot oil (375°), cooking only a few at a time. Fry until hush puppies are golden brown. Drain well on paper towels. Yield: about 2½ dozen.

BOONE TAVERN HUSH PUPPIES

¼ teaspoon baking soda
½ cup buttermilk
1 cup cornmeal
½ teaspoon baking
  powder
½ teaspoon salt
1 egg, beaten
½ cup finely chopped
  onion
Vegetable oil

Dissolve soda in buttermilk; stir well. Combine cornmeal, baking powder, and salt. Stir in buttermilk mixture, egg, and onion, mixing well.

Carefully drop batter by tablespoonfuls into deep, hot oil (350°), cooking only a few at a time. Fry for 3 minutes or until hush puppies are golden brown, turning once. Drain well on paper towels. Yield: about 1½ dozen.

MARYLAND FRIED MUSH

1 cup cornmeal
1 cup cold water
1½ teaspoons salt
3 cups boiling water
About 2 cups all-purpose flour
Vegetable oil

Combine cornmeal and cold water; stir well. Dissolve salt in boiling water in top of double boiler; add cornmeal mixture, and cook over boiling water 30 minutes, stirring occasionally. Remove from heat, and spread mixture evenly into a lightly greased 15- x 10- x 1-inch jelly-roll pan. Cool 30 minutes.

Cut mush with assorted 2-inch cookie cutters, and sprinkle lightly with flour. Heat 2 inches of oil in a large skillet to 375°; add mush, and fry 5 minutes or until golden brown, turning once. Yield: 2½ dozen.

The origin of spoonbread is unclear, but one conjecture is that a seasoned cook found a heap of mush left over from breakfast. In the best Southern tradition, she simply added eggs, milk, and leavening, baked it, and served it up with a spoon as a side dish for supper.

Whatever the story, there are varied recipes for spoonbread throughout the South. A spoonbread containing grits is called, unaccountably, Ovendaugh, Owendaw, or Awendaw. And one of the loveliest is spoonbread with egg whites folded in to make a heavenly soufflé.

Mush and milk for supper. Lewis Miller sketch, 1809.

SERVED WITH A SPOON

SOUTH CAROLINA OVENDAUGH

1 cup uncooked instant grits
3 cups water
1 teaspoon salt
1 tablespoon butter or
  margarine
2 cups cornmeal
2 eggs, beaten
2 cups milk

Combine grits, water, and salt in a large saucepan; cook over medium heat 20 minutes, stirring occasionally. Remove from heat, and stir in butter. Add cornmeal, stirring well. Set aside to cool 10 minutes.

Stir eggs into cooled mixture. Gradually add milk, stirring well. Spoon batter into a lightly greased 2-quart baking dish. Bake at 350° for 1 hour and 5 minutes or until a knife inserted in center comes out clean. Yield: 8 servings.

AWENDAW

2 cups hot cooked hominy
  grits
1 tablespoon lard
1 teaspoon salt
2 cups milk
4 eggs, beaten
1 cup sifted cornmeal

Combine hot grits, lard, and salt, stirring until lard is melted. Gradually stir in remaining ingredients, mixing until well blended.

Pour batter into a lightly greased 2-quart casserole. Bake at 325° for 1 hour or until a knife inserted in center comes out clean. Yield: 8 servings.

Awendaw: For spooning up.

SOUTHERN SPOONBREAD

1 cup cornmeal
3 cups milk, scalded
4 eggs, separated
1 cup milk
2 tablespoons butter or
  margarine, softened
2 teaspoons baking powder
1 teaspoon salt

Combine cornmeal and scalded milk in top of double boiler, mixing well. Stir in egg yolks and 1 cup milk. Place over boiling water; cook, stirring constantly, until mixture reaches the consistency of mush. Remove from heat, and stir in butter, baking powder, and salt.

Beat egg whites (at room temperature) until stiff peaks form; fold into cornmeal mixture. Spoon into a greased 2-quart casserole. Bake at 400° for 35 minutes or until a knife inserted in center comes out clean. Serve immediately. Yield: 8 servings.

LUNCHEON SPOONBREAD

6 slices bacon
1 cup self-rising cornmeal
3 cups milk, scalded
¼ cup chopped onion
¼ cup chopped green
  pepper
4 eggs, separated
1½ cups (6 ounces) shredded
  sharp Cheddar cheese

Cook bacon in a large skillet until crisp. Remove bacon; reserve 2 tablespoons drippings. Crumble bacon; set aside.

Combine cornmeal and milk in a large mixing bowl; stir until mixture is the consistency of mush. Add bacon, onion, green pepper, and reserved bacon drippings, stirring well.

Beat egg yolks well; stir egg yolks and cheese into warm mixture.

Beat egg whites (at room temperature) until stiff peaks form; fold into cornmeal mixture. Spoon batter into 6 lightly greased 10-ounce custard cups. Bake at 350° for 30 minutes or until a knife inserted in the center comes out clean. Yield: 6 servings.

For a meal, add salad to Luncheon Spoonbread.

PARMESAN SPOONBREAD

1 cup cornmeal
½ cup grated Parmesan
  cheese
2 cups milk, scalded
4 eggs, separated
1 tablespoon butter or
  margarine, softened
2 teaspoons sugar
½ teaspoon salt

Combine cornmeal, cheese, and milk in top of a double boiler. Place over boiling water, and cook, stirring constantly, until mixture reaches the consistency of mush. Remove from heat, and cool slightly. Beat egg yolks well. Stir in yolks, butter, sugar, and salt, mixing well.

Beat egg whites (at room temperature) until stiff peaks form; fold into cornmeal mixture. Spoon into a lightly greased 2-quart casserole. Bake at 375° for 30 minutes or until a knife inserted in center comes out clean. Yield: 8 servings.

INDIVIDUAL SPOONBREADS

1 cup cornmeal
2 cups boiling water
¾ teaspoon salt
3 tablespoons butter or
  margarine
4 eggs
1 cup milk

Combine cornmeal, boiling water, and salt in a medium saucepan; cook over medium heat 1 minute or until thickened, stirring constantly. Remove from heat. Add butter, stirring until melted.

Beat eggs until thick and lemon colored. Gradually stir about one-fourth of hot mixture into eggs; add to remaining hot mixture, stirring constantly. Add milk, stirring until batter is smooth.

Pour into 6 lightly greased 10-ounce custard cups. Bake at 425° for 25 minutes or until a knife inserted in center comes out clean. Yield: 6 servings.

The Hotel Roanoke, Virginia's oasis of splendor since 1882.

The Hotel Roanoke presides over its quiet town in Southwest Virginia like a grand dame who has adjusted her skirts and settled in for a lengthy stay. One of the last independently-owned grand hotels, the Roanoke was built in 1882 by the Norfolk and Western Railroad, back when railroads did such things. Being small by modern standards, only 425 rooms, does not disturb her serenity, as she does not measure by modern terms.

It is not merely the crispness of the napery and the freshness of the flowers in the opulent dining room that bewitch the guest. It is the quality of the food that is put before him with genuine solicitude. And if one had to choose one *crème de la crème* dish to remember longest and best, it might be the Roanoke's spoonbread. It is frequently met with sighs of delight and near disbelief.

HOTEL ROANOKE SPOONBREAD

1½ cups water
¼ cup butter or margarine, softened
1 teaspoon sugar
1 teaspoon salt
1 cup cornmeal
1 teaspoon baking powder
5 eggs, beaten
2 cups milk

Combine water, butter, sugar, and salt in a medium saucepan; bring to a boil. Stir in cornmeal; boil 1 minute or until thickened, stirring constantly. Remove from heat. Add baking powder, eggs, and milk, stirring until well blended.

Pour batter into a lightly greased 2-quart casserole. Bake at 375° for 50 minutes or until a knife inserted in center comes out clean. Yield: 8 servings.

World War I promotion for corn in healthful guises, from hominy to cornmeal.

DIXIE SPOONBREAD

1 cup cornmeal
1 cup water
2 cups milk, divided
1 tablespoon butter or
    margarine, melted
2 teaspoons baking
    powder
1 teaspoon salt
2 eggs, separated

Combine cornmeal, water, and 1 cup milk in a medium saucepan; stir until blended. Cook over low heat until mixture is the consistency of mush. Remove from heat; add butter, baking powder, salt, and remaining milk. Beat egg yolks well; stir into warm mixture.

Beat egg whites (at room temperature) until stiff peaks form; fold into cornmeal mixture. Spoon into a greased 1½-quart casserole. Bake at 350° for 45 minutes or until a knife inserted in center comes out clean. Serve immediately. Yield: 4 to 6 servings.

EGG BREAD

2 eggs, beaten
2 cups buttermilk
1 tablespoon shortening,
    melted
1 cup sifted cornmeal
1 teaspoon baking soda
1 tablespoon sugar
1 teaspoon salt
2 cups milk

Combine first 7 ingredients; stir in milk. Heat a well-greased 9-inch cast-iron skillet in a 350° oven for 5 minutes or until very hot. Pour batter into hot skillet. Bake at 350° for 1 hour or until a knife inserted in center comes out clean. Yield: 6 to 8 servings.

LOUISIANA SPIDER BREAD

1½ cups cornmeal
⅓ cup sifted all-purpose
    flour
1 teaspoon baking soda
1 tablespoon sugar
1 teaspoon salt
2 tablespoons shortening,
    melted
2 eggs, beaten
1 cup buttermilk
2 cups milk, divided

Combine dry ingredients; add shortening, eggs, buttermilk, and 1 cup milk, mixing well.

Pour batter into a lightly greased 2-quart casserole. Pour remaining milk over batter in casserole; do not stir. Bake at 350° for 30 minutes or until a knife inserted in center comes out clean. Yield: 8 servings.

In the sixteenth century, cast iron was first used for fireplace furniture such as andirons and firebacks. Later, blacksmiths made some cookware, but by the 1800s, Northern factories were turning out skillets (spiders), pots, mortars, and kettles. Some spiders had three legs and some were fitted with concave lids. Often, the spider was placed "down-hearth," with hot coals underneath, the inside was greased, and spoonbread batter was poured in. The lid was then heaped with hot coals.

Hot coals on the lid allow Spider Bread to bake evenly.

BREADS ON THE RISE

Yeast, our oldest leavening, has been with us since ancient Egyptian breweries and bakeries were built side by side. A slurry containing wild yeast from fermenting grain in the brewers' vats was carried over to the baker, who added it to his breadstuffs. The dough rose, for some reason, and bread was baked. The consumer came to the baker; bread was not baked at home.

Animal, vegetable, or mineral? Yeast is a plant, and there are varieties, just as there are kinds of beans. Modern yeast is grown in a molasses medium, as yeast feeds only on simple sugars. We buy it as cake yeast or active dry yeast. Many prefer the latter for its longer shelf life and higher tolerance for heat in the proofing.

Away from brewers' vats, our forebears made yeast from hops, potatoes, malt, even peach leaves—anything that could be fermented and mixed with flour. A starter had to be kept going, as it was a time-consuming nuisance to make a new one. The apocryphal story of the "Sourdough" miner whose pack mule fell over a cliff illustrates the value of the starter on the frontier: As his friends restrained him from climbing down the precipice, he cried, "I know the mule's dead, men. My starter's in my saddlebags."

Many cooks still labor under the impression that yeast is a difficult ingredient. This chapter should lay that fear to rest. The novice will realize there are a few simple truths that become clearer with each baking. First, yeast is dormant below about 50° F; therefore, refrigerate it until ready to use. Heat higher than 120° F kills yeast; just as you would not water plants with hot water, use tap water no warmer than 110° to 115° F for dry yeast, 100° F for cake yeast.

Always proof ("prove") the yeast: Stir it into the warm liquid with the finger to start it dissolving; then set the container in a pan of warm water. While a pinch of sugar feeds the yeast and speeds the proofing, too much sugar retards yeast development, as does salt. Some "old wives tales" are true: a tiny pinch, not enough to taste, of spice, such as cinnamon or ginger or nutmeg, does speed yeast development, according to food chemists.

Yeast baking, as we accumulate experience, is more fun than most other cooking!

Breads from the Hermann-Grima kitchen, clockwise from left: Sausage in Brioche, Round Crusty Loaf, New Orleans French Bread, Round French Bread being drawn from oven, Traditional Brioche, Brioche with Cheese, and sliced Round Crusty Loaf.

SHAKER FRIENDSHIP BREAD

2 cups Sourdough Starter (at
room temperature)
1½ cups water
½ cup vegetable oil
⅓ cup sugar
1 tablespoon salt
7 cups all-purpose flour
Melted butter or margarine

Combine Sourdough Starter,
water, oil, sugar, salt, and 3
cups flour in a large mixing
bowl; beat with an electric mixer
until smooth. Stir in enough remaining flour to make a soft
dough.

Turn dough out onto a floured
surface, and knead 10 minutes
or until smooth and elastic.
Place dough in a greased bowl,
turning to grease top. Cover and
let rise 6 hours or until doubled
in bulk.

Punch dough down; turn out
onto a lightly floured surface.
Divide in half, shaping each half
into a loaf. Cover and let rest 5
minutes. Place loaves in 2
greased 9- x 5- x 3-inch loafpans. Cover and repeat rising
procedure 3 hours or until doubled in bulk. Place in a cold
oven. Bake at 350° for 40 minutes or until loaves sound hollow when tapped. Remove bread
from pans, and cool on wire
racks. Brush tops with melted
butter. Yield: 2 loaves.

*Friendship Bread (right) and Salt-Rising
Bread in Shakertown kitchen.*

Sourdough Starter:

1 package dry yeast
3 cups warm water (105° to
115°), divided
2 cups all-purpose flour,
sifted
2 tablespoons sugar
Starter Food

Dissolve yeast in ½ cup warm
water, stirring well; let stand 5
minutes or until bubbly.

Combine remaining water,
flour, and sugar in a medium-
size, nonmetal bowl; mix well.

Add dissolved yeast, and stir
well. Cover loosely with plastic
wrap or cheesecloth, and let
stand in a warm place (80° to
85°) for 72 hours, stirring 2 to 3
times daily. Place fermented
mixture in refrigerator, and stir
daily; use within 11 days.

To use, let Sourdough Starter
stand at room temperature at
least 1 hour. Stir well, and measure amount of starter needed
for recipe. Replenish remaining
starter with Starter Food, and
return to refrigerator; use

within 2 to 11 days, stirring
daily.

Repeat procedure for using
and replenishing Sourdough
Starter. Yield: about 2 cups.

Starter Food:

2 cups all-purpose flour,
sifted
½ cup sugar
1½ cups water

Stir all ingredients into remaining Sourdough Starter,
and refrigerate.

SHAKER SALT-RISING BREAD

1 cup milk, scalded
¼ cup plus 3 tablespoons
  cornmeal
¼ teaspoon baking soda,
  divided
1 tablespoon plus ½
  teaspoon sugar,
  divided
1¾ teaspoons salt, divided
8½ cups all-purpose flour,
  divided
1¾ cups warm water (105° to
  115°), divided
½ cup shortening
Melted butter or margarine

Combine milk, cornmeal, ⅛ teaspoon soda, ½ teaspoon sugar, and ¼ teaspoon salt in a medium-size mixing bowl. Cover tightly wih plastic wrap, and place in a lighted warm place (80° to 85°) for 72 hours. (Batter will become puffy and bubbly over the fermentation period.)

Add 2½ cups flour, 1 cup warm water, remaining soda, and ½ teaspoon salt to fermented starter; stir well. Cover and let rise in a warm place (85°), free from drafts, 4 hours or until doubled in bulk.

Combine remaining flour, sugar, and salt in a large mixing bowl. Cut in shortening until mixture resembles coarse meal. Add remaining warm water and risen starter mixture; stir until dough leaves sides of bowl. Turn dough out onto a lightly floured surface, and knead 8 minutes or until dough is smooth. Dough will be stiff.

Divide dough into 3 equal portions, shaping each into a loaf. Place in 3 greased 7½- x 3- x 2-inch loafpans. Brush loaves with melted butter. Cover and let rise in a warm place (85°), free from drafts, 3 hours or until doubled in bulk. Bake at 325° for 10 minutes; increase temperature to 350°, and bake an additional 40 minutes or until loaves sound hollow when tapped. Remove bread from pans immediately; cool on wire racks. Yield: 3 loaves.

Lot's wife, sculpted in salt, displayed at the New Orleans Exposition of 1884.

The interest a baker takes in the time-consuming process of naturally-fermented bread baking may be a measure of his patience and perseverance. Self-starters do not always start the first time, even though one follows directions. Our modern milk may be responsible. The recipes originated during the days when milk used was not pasteurized, so the ferment developed more quickly. Our modern pasteurized, homogenized milk will sometimes spoil before it sours.

Whatever the reason, salt-rising bread made without a yeast starter may frustrate even the most accomplished cook—and may not be worth it to some. People tend to regard salt-rising bread either with adoration or utter contempt. If you adore it, it is worth every minute. Sourdough lovers, once a starter is established, are in for a lifetime, literally, of good things, as the starter can be kept alive and working for many years.

Working yeast, tightly sealed, will pop its cork eventually.

FOOLPROOF SALT-RISING BREAD

¼ cup vegetable oil
8 to 8¼ cups all-purpose flour
2 teaspoons salt
4 cups Potato-Yeast Starter

Stir oil, flour, and salt into Potato-Yeast Starter (dough will be moderately stiff). Spoon dough into a large greased bowl; cover and let rise in a warm place (85°), free from drafts, 1½ hours or until doubled in bulk.

Stir dough down. Divide into 3 equal portions and place in 3 greased 9- x 5- x 3-inch loafpans or 1-quart casseroles. Cover and let rise in a warm place, free from drafts, until doubled in bulk. Bake at 375° for 50 to 60 minutes or until loaves sound hollow when tapped. Remove bread from pans; cool on wire racks. Yield: 3 loaves.

Potato-Yeast Starter:

3 medium potatoes, peeled and cubed
6 cups water
½ cup all-purpose flour
2 tablespoons sugar
2 packages dry yeast
½ cup sugar
2 tablespoons sugar

Combine potatoes and water in a Dutch oven; cover and cook 10 to 15 minutes or until potatoes are tender. Drain, reserving 5 cups potato liquid. Reserve potatoes for other uses.

Allow 1 cup potato liquid to cool to 120° to 130°. Combine flour, 2 tablespoons sugar, and

yeast in a large bowl; stir in the 1 cup cooled potato liquid. Cover and let stand in a warm place (85°) for 4 hours. Stir in remaining 4 cups potato liquid and ½ cup sugar. Cover and let mixture stand in a warm place overnight.

Stir starter well; reserve 1 cup. Stir 2 tablespoons sugar into reserved 1 cup starter, and pour into an airtight 2-cup glass container. Store in refrigerator until ready to use for second batch of bread.

Use remaining 4 cups starter to make Foolproof Salt-Rising Bread. Yield: 5 cups.

Note: To make a second batch of bread, use reserved 1 cup starter plus 3 cups plain potato water to equal 4 cups starter.

SOURDOUGH BREAD

2 tablespoons sugar
2 tablespoons shortening, melted
1 teaspoon salt
2½ cups Sourdough Starter (at room temperature)
2½ cups all-purpose flour
2 tablespoons cornmeal

Combine sugar, shortening, and salt in a large mixing bowl; add Sourdough Starter, and stir until sugar dissolves.

Gradually add flour, stirring until dough leaves sides of bowl. Turn dough out onto a heavily floured surface; knead 10 minutes or until smooth and elastic. Place dough in a greased bowl, turning to grease top. Cover and

let rise in a warm place (85°), free from drafts, 1 hour or until doubled in bulk (dough will be sticky). Punch dough down, and let rest 5 minutes. Turn dough out onto a floured surface; divide in half.

Grease a baking sheet; sprinkle with cornmeal. Set aside.

Roll each half into a 12- x 10-inch rectangle. Roll up jellyroll fashion, beginning at wide edge. Place dough, seam side down, on baking sheet; turn edges under. Cover and repeat rising procedure 25 minutes or until doubled in bulk.

Cut several diagonal slashes, ¾-inch deep, in top of each loaf. Bake at 400° for 30 minutes or until loaves sound hollow when tapped. Remove to wire racks to cool. Yield: 2 loaves.

Sourdough Starter:

2 packages dry yeast
2 tablespoons sugar
4 cups warm water (105° to 115°), divided
4 cups all-purpose flour

Dissolve yeast and sugar in 1 cup warm water in a medium-size nonmetal bowl, stirring well. Let stand 5 minutes or until bubbly. Gradually add remaining warm water and flour; mix well. Cover loosely with plastic wrap or cheesecloth, and let stand in a warm place (85°), free from drafts, 10 to 12 hours. Place fermented mixture in refrigerator, and stir daily; use within 11 days.

To use, let Sourdough Starter stand at room temperature at least 1 hour. Stir well; measure amount of starter needed for recipe, reserving ½ cup.

Add 2 cups all-purpose flour and 2 cups warm water (105° to 115°) to reserved starter; mix well and refrigerate.

Repeat this procedure for using and replenishing Sourdough Starter as needed. Yield: about 5 cups.

Bread baking was once an all-day task. Here a conscientious cook readies another loaf for the pan.

FROM LIGHT TO DARK

BASIC WHITE BREAD

1 package dry yeast
1 teaspoon sugar
1 cup warm water (105° to 115°)
1½ tablespoons sugar
1 teaspoon salt
2 tablespoons vegetable oil
2¾ to 3 cups all-purpose flour,
    divided
Melted butter or margarine

Dissolve yeast and 1 teaspoon sugar in warm water. Stir well; cover and let stand at room temperature 5 minutes or until bubbly. Combine yeast mixture, 1½ tablespoons sugar, salt, oil, and half the flour in a large mixing bowl. Beat mixture at low speed of an electric mixer until smooth. Stir in enough remaining flour to make a soft dough.

Turn dough out onto a lightly floured surface and knead 8 minutes or until smooth and elastic. Place dough in a greased bowl, turning to grease top. Cover and let rise in a warm place (85°), free from drafts, 1½ hours or until doubled in bulk.

Punch dough down. Turn out onto a floured surface; let rest 15 minutes.

Roll dough into a 14- x 7-inch rectangle. Beginning at narrow edge, roll up dough; press firmly to eliminate air pockets. Pinch edges to seal. Place dough, seam side down, in a well-greased 9- x 5- x 3-inch loafpan. Cover and repeat rising procedure 1 hour or until doubled in bulk. Bake at 375° for 50 minutes or until loaf sounds hollow when tapped. Remove bread from pan immediately; cool on wire rack. Brush with melted butter. Yield: 1 loaf.

THE UNIFORM BREAD SLICER

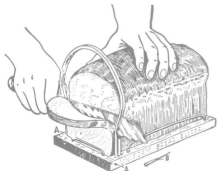

[PATENT APPLIED FOR]

Step 1—Pour dissolved yeast mixture into dry ingredients; mix thoroughly, adding enough remaining flour to make a soft dough.

Step 4—Shape into loaf by rolling dough into a rectangle. Gently roll up jellyroll fashion, starting at short side.

Step 2—Turn dough out onto a lightly floured surface; knead 8 minutes or until smooth and elastic, using the heel of the hand to work the dough.

Step 3—Place dough in a greased bowl; cover and let rise in a warm place (85°), until doubled in bulk. Dough has doubled in bulk if indentations remain in dough when pressed with fingers.

Step 5—Shape the roll, gently folding the ends of the dough under to form a rounded loaf.

Step 6—Place shaped loaf into a greased baking pan, pressing dough to conform to shape of pan.

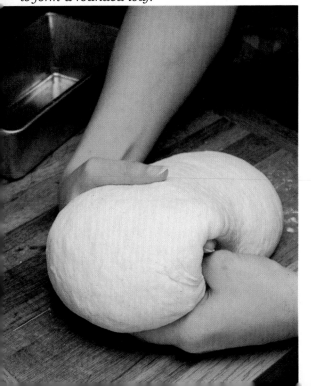

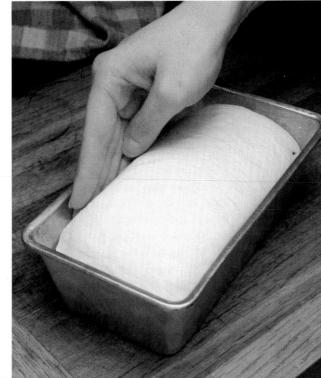

Shakertown at Pleasant Hill, Kentucky, with 27 restored buildings on 2250 acres.

SHAKER DAILY LOAF

2 packages dry yeast
¼ cup warm water (105° to 115°)
2 cups milk
½ cup shortening
¼ cup sugar
1 tablespoon plus 1 teaspoon salt
2 cups water
9 to 11 cups sifted bread flour

Dissolve yeast in warm water, stirring well; let stand 5 minutes or until bubbly.

Scald milk; add shortening, sugar, and salt, stirring until shortening is melted. Add water; let cool until mixture is lukewarm (105° to 115°). Stir in dissolved yeast. Gradually stir in enough flour to make a soft dough.

Turn dough out onto a heavily floured surface, and knead 8 minutes or until smooth and elastic. Place dough in a greased bowl, turning to grease top. Cover and let rise in a warm place (85°), free from drafts, 1 hour or until doubled in bulk.

Punch dough down; turn out onto a floured surface. Divide into 4 equal portions, shaping each into a smooth ball. Cover; let rest 10 minutes.

Shape each portion into a loaf; place in 4 greased 8½- x 4½- x 2½-inch loafpans. Cover and repeat rising procedure 45 minutes or until doubled in bulk. Bake at 375° for 35 minutes or until loaves sound hollow when tapped. Remove bread from pans immediately; cool on wire racks. Yield: 4 loaves.

IRISH BREAD

1 cup milk
1 package dry yeast
1 teaspoon sugar
2 tablespoons butter or
  margarine, melted
1 egg, beaten
2 cups sifted all-purpose flour
½ teaspoon salt
Butter or margarine

Scald milk, and cool to luke-warm (105° to 115°). Dissolve yeast and sugar in milk; stir well, and let stand 5 minutes or until bubbly. Add 2 tablespoons melted butter and egg, beating well. Stir in flour and salt, beating until smooth.

Pour batter into a well-greased 8-inch cast-iron skillet. Let rise in a warm place (85°), free from drafts, 45 minutes or until doubled in bulk. Bake at 350° for 30 minutes. Remove bread from skillet immediately, and place on wire rack.

Cut bread in half horizontally, and spread bottom layer with butter. Cover with top layer, and cut into wedges to serve. Yield: 8 servings.

IVY NECK LIGHT BREAD

2 packages dry yeast
3¼ cups warm water (105° to
  115°), divided
9 cups all-purpose flour
¼ cup plus 1½ teaspoons
  sugar
2 tablespoons salt
3 tablespoons lard

Dissolve yeast in 1 cup warm water, stirring well; let stand 5 minutes or until bubbly.

Sift flour, sugar, and salt into a large bowl. Cut in lard until mixture resembles coarse meal. Add dissolved yeast to dry ingredients; stir well. Add remaining warm water; stir well.

Turn dough out onto a lightly floured surface; knead 10 minutes or until smooth and elastic. Place dough in a greased bowl, turning to grease top. Cover and let rise in a warm place (85°), free from drafts, 1 hour or until doubled in bulk.

Punch dough down, and turn out onto a floured surface. Knead dough 3 to 4 times or until smooth and elastic. Cover; let rest 10 minutes.

Divide dough into 4 equal portions, shaping each portion into a loaf. Place in 4 greased 7½- x 3- x 2-inch loafpans. Cover and repeat rising procedure 40 minutes or until doubled in bulk. Bake at 400° for 45 minutes or until loaves sound hollow when tapped. Remove bread from pans immediately; cool on wire racks. Yield: 4 loaves.

*Indians of the Southwest
had adobe ovens
long before other tribes (or
settlers) in America.*

ADOBE OVEN BREAD

1 package dry yeast
½ cup warm water (105° to
  115°)
¼ cup plus 1 tablespoon
  shortening, melted
2¼ teaspoons salt
6½ to 7½ cups all-purpose
  flour, divided
2 cups water

Dissolve yeast in warm water in a large mixing bowl, stirring well. Let stand 5 minutes or until bubbly. Stir in shortening and salt. Add 6 cups flour alternately with 2 cups water, beginning and ending with flour. Gradually stir in enough remaining flour to make a soft dough. Shape into a ball.

Place dough in a greased bowl, turning to grease top. Cover and let rise in a warm place (85°), free from drafts, 1 hour or until doubled in bulk.

Punch dough down; turn out onto a lightly floured surface. Knead 6 minutes or until smooth and elastic. Cover and let dough rest 10 minutes.

Divide dough in half, and shape each into a loaf. Place in 2 greased 8½- x 4½- x 3-inch loafpans. Cover and repeat rising procedure 20 minutes. Cut 2 diagonal slashes, ¾-inch deep, in top of each loaf. Bake at 400° for 50 minutes or until loaves sound hollow when tapped. Remove bread from pans immediately; cool on wire racks. Yield: 2 loaves.

Eye-catching early 1900s advertisement for yeast.

NEW ORLEANS FRENCH BREAD

1 package dry yeast
2½ cups warm water (105° to 115°)
2 tablespoons sugar, divided
1 tablespoon salt
6½ to 7 cups all-purpose flour, divided
1 egg white, slightly beaten

Combine yeast, water, and 1 teaspoon sugar in a large bowl, stirring until dissolved. Stir in remaining sugar, salt, and 6 cups flour to form a stiff dough.

Turn dough out onto a surface sprinkled with remaining flour; knead 8 minutes or until smooth and elastic. Place dough in a greased bowl, turning to grease top. Cover and let rise in a warm place (85°), free from drafts, 1½ hours or until doubled in bulk. Turn dough out onto a lightly floured surface. Cover and let rest 15 minutes. Knead 3 to 4 times.

Divide dough into 4 equal portions; roll each portion into a 13- x 7-inch rectangle. Roll up each rectangle jellyroll fashion, starting at long end. Pinch seams and ends together to seal. Place loaves, seam side down, in 4 heavily-greased baguette pans or on baking sheets.

Cut 3 or 4 diagonal slashes, ¾-inch deep, in top of each loaf. Cover and repeat rising procedure 1 hour or until doubled in bulk. Brush loaves with egg white. Bake at 450° for 15 minutes; reduce heat to 350°, and bake 30 minutes or until loaves sound hollow when tapped. Remove bread from pans or baking sheets immediately; cool on wire racks. Yield: 4 loaves.

EGG LIGHT BREAD

2 packages dry yeast
½ cup sugar, divided
½ cup warm water (105° to 115°)
2 cups milk, scalded
½ cup shortening
1 teaspoon salt
2 egg whites
7¼ cups all-purpose flour, divided

Combine yeast, 1 teaspoon sugar, and warm water in a mixing bowl; stir well. Let stand 5 minutes or until bubbly.

Combine milk, shortening, salt, and remaining sugar; stir until shortening is melted. Add cooled milk mixture to yeast mixture; stir well. Beat egg whites (at room temperature) until stiff peaks form; fold into yeast mixture.

Gradually add 6 cups flour, stirring until dough leaves sides of bowl. Shape into a ball, and place in a greased bowl, turning to grease top. Cover and let rise in a warm place (85°), free from drafts, 1 hour or until doubled in bulk. Punch dough down, and turn out onto a lightly floured surface. Let dough rest 5 minutes.

Knead remaining flour into dough. Shape into a ball; place in a greased bowl. Cover and repeat rising procedure 1 hour or until doubled in bulk.

Punch dough down; turn out onto a lightly floured surface, and knead 4 to 5 times. Let dough rest 5 minutes.

Divide dough in half, shaping each into a loaf. Place in 2 greased 9- x 5- x 3-inch loaf-pans. Cover and repeat rising procedure 30 minutes. Bake at 350° for 35 minutes or until loaves sound hollow when tapped. Remove bread from pans immediately; cool on wire racks. Yield: 2 loaves.

SWISS EGG BRAID

4 cups milk
2 packages dry yeast
⅓ cup warm water (105° to 115°)
½ cup plus 2 tablespoons
  sugar, divided
14½ to 15 cups all-purpose
  flour, divided
6 eggs, beaten
1 cup shortening, melted
2 teaspoons salt
1 egg yolk
1 teaspoon water
Butter or margarine, melted

Scald milk; let cool to luke-warm (105° to 115°). Dissolve yeast in warm water; let stand 5 minutes or until bubbly.

Combine milk, dissolved yeast, 2 tablespoons sugar, and 3 cups flour in a large bowl; stir well. Cover and let rise in a warm place (85°), free from drafts, 1 hour or until doubled in bulk.

Stir mixture down. Add 4 cups flour, remaining ½ cup sugar, eggs, shortening, and salt; mix well. Gradually stir in enough remaining flour to make a stiff dough.

Turn dough out onto a floured surface; knead 10 minutes. Place in a greased bowl, turning to grease top; cover.

Let dough rise in a warm place (85°), free from drafts, 1 hour or until doubled in bulk. Punch dough down; cover and let rest 10 minutes.

Divide dough into 4 equal por-tions. Divide each portion into 3 equal pieces. Shape each piece into a 12-inch rope. Braid ropes, pinching ends to seal. Place braided loaf in a greased 9- x 5- x 3-inch loafpan. Repeat procedure with remaining 3 portions of dough.

Cover and repeat rising proce-dure 1 hour or until doubled in bulk. Combine egg yolk and water; beat well, and gently brush over top of loaves. Bake at 325° for 45 minutes or until loaves sound hollow when tapped. Remove bread from pans immediately; cool on wire racks. Brush with melted but-ter. Yield: 4 loaves.

NEIMAN-MARCUS MONKEY BREAD

1 cup milk
½ cup butter or margarine
¼ cup sugar
1 teaspoon salt
1 package dry yeast
3½ cups all-purpose flour
½ cup butter or margarine,
  melted

Combine milk, ½ cup butter, sugar, and salt in a saucepan; heat until butter melts. Cool to 105° to 115°; add yeast, stirring until dissolved. Place flour in a large bowl; add milk mixture, and stir until well blended.

Cover and let rise in a warm place (85°), free from drafts, 1 hour and 20 minutes or until doubled in bulk. Punch dough down. Roll dough into 1½-inch balls; dip each ball in melted butter.

Layer balls of dough in a 10-inch tube or Bundt pan. Cover and repeat rising procedure 45 minutes or until doubled in bulk. Bake at 375° for 35 min-utes. Cool in pan 5 minutes; in-vert onto serving plate. Yield: one 10-inch loaf.

Swiss Egg Braid: The shaping and result are irresistible.

HERMANN-GRIMA BRIOCHE

3 packages dry yeast
1 tablespoon sugar
½ cup warm water (105° to 115°)
2 cups milk
½ cup unsalted butter
3 tablespoons sugar
1 tablespoon salt
3 eggs, beaten
8 cups all-purpose flour, divided

Dissolve yeast and 1 tablespoon sugar in warm water; stir well, and let stand 5 minutes or until bubbly.

Scald milk; add butter, 3 tablespoons sugar, and salt. Stir until butter melts. Let mixture cool to lukewarm (105° to 115°).

Combine yeast mixture, milk mixture, eggs, and 2 cups flour; beat with an electric mixer until smooth. Cover and let rise in a warm place (85°), free from drafts, 1½ hours.

Stir mixture; add enough remaining flour to make a soft dough. Turn dough out onto a heavily floured surface, and knead 10 minutes or until smooth and elastic.

Place in a well-greased bowl, turning to grease top. Cover and repeat rising procedure 1 hour or until doubled in bulk.

Punch dough down. Divide dough into 3 equal portions; shape and bake as directed.

Basic Brioche:

1 portion Hermann-Grima Brioche dough
1 egg yolk, beaten
2 teaspoons milk

Cut off one-third of dough; set aside. Lightly knead larger portion of dough 4 to 5 times; shape into a ball, and place in a well-greased 5 cup brioche mold. Shape smaller reserved portion of dough into a ball, rolling one end to form a tapered, teardrop shape. Set aside.

Using three floured fingers, press down into center of dough in brioche mold, touching bottom of mold. Enlarge this cavity to shape of tapered end of reserved dough ball. Place tapered end into cavity, rounding upper portion of teardrop to form a smooth ball. Cover and repeat rising procedure 1 hour or until doubled in bulk.

Combine egg yolk and milk, stirring well. Lightly brush mixture over top of brioche. Bake at 350° for 45 minutes or until golden brown. Remove bread from mold immediately; cool on wire rack. Yield: 1 loaf.

Brioche with Gruyère and Parmesan:

1 portion Hermann-Grima Brioche dough
¾ cup (3 ounces) shredded Gruyére cheese, divided
¼ cup grated Parmesan cheese, divided
1 egg yolk, beaten
2 teaspoons milk

Knead dough lightly 4 to 5 times, kneading in 6 tablespoons Gruyère cheese and 2 tablespoons Parmesan cheese.

Shape dough into an oval loaf; place on a greased baking sheet. Cover and let rise in a warm place (85°), free from drafts, 1 hour or until doubled in bulk.

Combine egg yolk and milk, stirring well; gently brush mixture over loaf. Sprinkle with remaining cheese. Bake at 350° for 45 minutes or until loaf sounds hollow when tapped. Cool on wire rack. Yield: 1 loaf.

Sausage in Brioche:

1 portion Hermann-Grima Brioche dough
1 (½ pound) cooked smoked kielbasa sausage link (about 6 to 7 inches long)
1 egg yolk, beaten
2 teaspoons milk

Roll dough into an 11- x 8-inch rectangle. Place sausage on short end of dough; roll up jellyroll fashion. Pinch seams and ends together to seal. Place roll, seam side down, in a greased 8½- x 4½- x 3-inch loafpan. Cover and let rise in a warm place (85°), free from drafts, 1 hour or until doubled in bulk.

Combine egg yolk and milk; stir well. Gently brush mixture over top of loaf. Bake at 350° for 45 minutes or until loaf sounds hollow when tapped. Remove bread from pan; cool on wire rack. Yield: 1 loaf.

The "tomorrow" kitchen of the Hermann-Grima House in 1830: A fireplace for cooking and stew-holes besides!

Ph. Hoelzel's mill in New Orleans could grind any grain.

TRADITIONAL BRIOCHE

2 cups sifted all-purpose
  flour, divided
1 package dry yeast
3¼ cups warm water (105°
  to 115°), divided
1 tablespoon sugar
1 teaspoon salt
2 eggs, slightly beaten
2 tablespoons milk
½ cup butter or margarine,
  softened
1 egg white, slightly
  beaten

Combine ½ cup flour and yeast; add ¼ cup warm water, stirring until dry ingredients are moistened and dough forms a soft ball. Make 2 crossed slashes, ¾-inch deep, in top of dough ball. Place dough ball in remaining warm water; set aside 5 minutes or until dough ball rises to surface. Remove dough from water, and place in a greased bowl. Cover and let rise in a warm place (85°), free from drafts, 1 hour or until doubled in bulk.

Combine remaining flour, sugar, and salt. Make a well in center of flour mixture, and stir in eggs and milk. Beat vigorously for 3 minutes or until mixture forms a smooth, shiny paste.

Cream butter; add butter and dough ball to paste, mixing thoroughly. Place in a well-greased bowl; cover tightly with plastic wrap, and refrigerate overnight.

Punch dough down, and turn out onto a lightly floured surface. Set one-third of dough aside; lightly knead together the remaining dough 4 to 5 times. Shape dough into a ball, and place in a well-greased 5 cup brioche mold.

Shape reserved portion of dough into a ball, rolling one end to form a tapered, teardrop shape. Set aside.

Using three floured fingers, press down into center of dough in brioche mold, touching bottom of mold. Enlarge this cavity to shape of tapered end of reserved dough ball. Place tapered end into cavity, rounding upper portion of teardrop to form a smooth ball. Cover and repeat rising procedure 1 hour or until doubled in bulk.

Bake at 375° for 30 minutes; lightly brush with egg white, and bake an additional 10 minutes or until golden brown. Remove bread from mold immediately; cool on wire rack. Yield: 1 loaf.

KENTUCKY SALLY LUNN

1½ packages dry yeast
¾ cup warm milk (105° to 115°)
¾ cup butter or margarine, softened
¼ cup plus 2 tablespoons sugar
3 eggs, separated
3 cups all-purpose flour
¾ teaspoon salt

Dissolve yeast in warm milk, stirring well. Let stand 5 minutes or until bubbly.

Cream butter; gradually add sugar, beating well. Add egg yolks, beating until smooth.

Combine flour and salt; add to creamed mixture alternately with yeast mixture, beginning and ending with flour mixture. Beat egg whites (at room temperature) until stiff peaks form; fold into batter.

Spoon batter into a well-greased 9-cup mold. Let rise, uncovered, in a warm place (85°), free from drafts, 1 hour or until doubled in bulk.

Bake at 375° for 30 minutes or until golden brown. Cool in mold 10 minutes; invert onto serving plate. Slice and serve. Yield: 10 to 12 servings.

NORTH CAROLINA SALLY LUNN

1 package dry yeast
1 cup warm milk (105° to 115°)
3 eggs, well beaten
4 cups all-purpose flour
2 tablespoons sugar
1 teaspoon salt
½ teaspoon baking soda
½ cup warm water (105° to 115°)
½ cup butter or margarine, melted

Dissolve yeast in warm milk, stirring well. Let stand 5 minutes or until bubbly.

Combine eggs, flour, sugar, and salt in a medium-size bowl; mix well. Dissolve soda in water, stirring well. Add soda mixture, butter, and dissolved yeast to flour mixture; mix well.

Spoon batter into a well-greased 10-inch tube pan. Cover and let rise in a warm place (85°), free from drafts, 2 hours or until doubled in bulk. Bake at 400° for 30 minutes or until a wooden pick inserted in middle of bread comes out clean. Remove bread from pan; place on wire rack to cool. Yield: one 10-inch loaf.

North Carolina Sally Lunn, delicious served with dinner; or try it toasted and buttered to go with tea.

Salem, North Carolina, home of the Winkler Bakery: Painted by C.D. Welfare, 1824.

WHOLE WHEAT BREAD

1 package dry yeast
1 tablespoon sugar, divided
2⅓ cups warm water (105° to 115°), divided
2 tablespoons shortening, softened
2 teaspoons salt
2 cups shreds of wheat bran cereal
4 to 5 cups all-purpose flour

Dissolve yeast and 1 teaspoon sugar in ⅓ cup warm water; stir well, and let stand 5 minutes.

Combine remaining sugar and warm water, shortening, and salt in a large mixing bowl; stir until shortening melts. Stir in yeast mixture, cereal, and enough flour to make a soft dough.

Turn dough out onto a lightly floured surface, and knead 10 minutes or until smooth and elastic. Place dough in a greased bowl, turning to grease top. Cover and let rise in a warm place (85°), free from drafts, 1 hour or until doubled in bulk. Punch dough down; cover and repeat rising procedure 1 hour or until doubled in bulk.

Turn dough out onto a lightly floured surface. Divide dough in half; cover and let rest 10 minutes. Shape into loaves and place in 2 greased 7½- x 3- x 2-inch loafpans. Cover and repeat rising procedure 1 hour or until doubled in bulk. Bake at 350° for 55 minutes or until loaves sound hollow when tapped. Remove bread from pans, and bake an additional 3 minutes to crisp bottoms of loaves. Cool on wire racks. Yield: 2 loaves.

WINKLER HONEY WHEAT BREAD

2¼ cups warm water (105° to 115°)
½ cup honey
3 tablespoons firmly packed brown sugar
2 packages dry yeast
1 cup instant nonfat dry milk powder
2 tablespoons shortening, melted
1 egg, beaten
1 teaspoon ground cumin
1 teaspoon salt
2 cups all-purpose flour
5 to 6 cups whole wheat flour

Combine water, honey, sugar, and yeast in a large bowl; stir well, and let stand 5 minutes or until bubbly. Stir in milk powder, shortening, egg, cumin, and salt. Add all-purpose flour, stirring with a wire whisk until mixture is smooth. Stir in enough whole wheat flour to make a soft dough.

Turn dough out onto a floured surface; knead 10 minutes or until smooth and elastic. Place in a greased bowl, turning to grease top. Cover and let rise in a warm place (85°), 1 hour or until doubled in bulk.

Punch dough down; turn out onto a lightly floured surface, and divide in half. Roll each half into a 13- x 8-inch rectangle. Beginning at narrow edge, roll up dough; press firmly to eliminate air pockets. Pinch edges to seal. Place loaves, seam side down, in 2 greased 9- x 5- x 3-inch loafpans. Cover and repeat rising procedure 1 hour or until doubled in bulk. Bake at 375° for 40 minutes or until loaves sound hollow when tapped. Remove bread from pans, and bake an additional 3 minutes to crisp bottom of loaves. Cool on wire racks. Yield: 2 loaves.

ROUND CRUSTY LOAF

2 packages dry yeast
½ cup sugar, divided
½ cup warm water (105°
  to 115°)
2 cups milk, scalded
1 cup unsalted butter,
  softened
1 teaspoon salt
4 eggs, beaten
2 cups whole wheat flour
6 cups bread flour
Cornmeal
1 egg yolk
1 teaspoon whipping cream

Dissolve yeast and 1 teaspoon sugar in warm water, stirring well; let stand 5 minutes or until bubbly.

Pour scalded milk over butter in a large mixing bowl; stir until butter has melted. Cool to lukewarm (105° to 115°). Add remaining sugar, yeast mixture, salt, and 4 eggs, stirring well. Gradually add whole wheat flour, beating well. Add enough bread flour to form a stiff dough.

Turn dough out onto a floured surface; knead 10 minutes or until smooth and elastic. Place in a greased bowl, turning to grease top. Cover and let rise in a warm place (85°), free from drafts, 1 hour and 15 minutes or until doubled in bulk.

Punch dough down; turn out onto a lightly floured surface. Let rest 5 minutes. Divide dough into 3 equal portions, shaping each portion into a round loaf. Place loaves on greased baking sheets sprinkled with cornmeal. Combine egg yolk and whipping cream; mix well, and lightly brush over top of loaves. Cover and repeat rising procedure 1 hour or until doubled in bulk.

Bake at 400° for 10 minutes; reduce temperature to 350°, and bake an additional 20 minutes or until loaves sound hollow when tapped. Remove bread from baking sheets; cool on wire racks. Yield: 3 round loaves.

Since 1931, the "Light Crust Doughboys" have been promoting Burrus Mill's flour in the Southwest. One alumnus, W.L. O'Daniel, became governor of Texas.

Burrus Milling Department, Division of Cargill, Inc.

Sylvester Graham

Sylvester Graham was a militant reformer years ahead of his time. He postulated a vegetarian diet, first as a cure for intemperance, then as a cure for what-ails-you. In addition to eating fresh fruits and vegetables, he made bread of unbolted wheat, wisely utilizing the richest part of the grain others were throwing away. Whole wheat flour, we call it sometimes. Graham attracted a number of imitators and cultists. At the same time, as his flour became more popular, there arose opportunists who blended bran with low-grade flour and marketed it as "graham flour." Graham lectured on the "science of human life" and published the collected lectures. He wrote books on bread as well. Fresh air while sleeping and loose, light clothing were part of his regimen. The man for whom the flour and the Graham cracker are named died in 1851 at the age of fifty-seven, presumably healthy as a horse.

GRAHAM BREAD

2 packages dry yeast
3 cups warm water (105° to 115°), divided
¼ cup firmly packed brown sugar
4 cups all-purpose flour
1 tablespoon salt
1 cup boiling water
½ cup butter or margarine
⅓ cup firmly packed brown sugar
6 to 7 cups whole wheat flour, divided
2 tablespoons butter or margarine, melted

Dissolve yeast in ¼ cup warm water in a large bowl; stir in ¼ cup brown sugar, and let stand 5 minutes.

Combine remaining warm water, all-purpose flour, and salt; stir into yeast mixture. Cover loosely with plastic wrap or cheesecloth, and let stand in a warm place (85°), free from drafts, 1½ hours.

Stir batter well; let rest 5 minutes. Combine boiling water, butter, and ⅓ cup brown sugar, stirring until butter is melted. Add butter mixture to batter; stir well. Add 4 cups whole wheat flour; stir until mixture is smooth. Stir in enough remaining whole wheat flour to form a moderately stiff dough.

Turn dough out onto a lightly floured surface; knead 8 minutes or until smooth and elastic. Place in a greased bowl, turning to grease top. Cover and let rise in a warm place, 1 hour or until doubled in bulk.

Punch dough down; turn out onto a lightly floured surface. Divide into 3 equal portions, shaping each into a smooth ball. Cover and let rest 10 minutes. Shape each portion into a loaf; place in 3 greased 9- x 5- x 3-inch loafpans. Cover and repeat rising procedure 40 minutes or until doubled in bulk. Bake at 375° for 45 minutes or until loaves sound hollow when tapped. Remove bread from pans immediately; cool on wire racks. Brush with melted butter. Yield: 3 loaves.

PUMPERNICKEL BREAD

6½ cups all-purpose flour
3 cups rye flour
1 cup shreds of wheat bran cereal
¾ cup yellow cornmeal
2 packages dry yeast
2 tablespoons salt
3½ cups water
¼ cup molasses
2 (1-ounce) squares unsweetened chocolate
1 tablespoon butter or margarine
2 cups cooked, mashed potatoes
2 teaspoons caraway seeds

Combine all-purpose and rye flour; stir well. Combine 2 cups flour mixture, cereal, cornmeal, yeast, and salt; mix well. Set remaining flour mixture aside.

Combine water, molasses, chocolate, and butter in a medium saucepan; heat mixture to 125°, stirring occasionally.

Gradually add hot liquid mixture to cereal mixture, beating at low speed of electric mixer 2 minutes. Add potatoes and 1 cup flour mixture; beat at high speed of electric mixer 2 minutes. Add caraway seeds and enough remaining flour mixture to form a soft dough, beating well after each addition.

Turn dough out onto a floured surface; cover and let rest 15 minutes. Knead 10 minutes or until smooth and elastic. Shape into a ball; place in a well-greased bowl, turning to grease top. Cover and let rise in a warm place (85°), free from drafts, 1 hour or until doubled in bulk.

Punch dough down; cover and repeat rising procedure 30 minutes. Punch dough down, and divide into 3 equal portions. Shape each portion into a ball. Place each ball in a greased 8-inch round cakepan. Cover and repeat rising procedure 45 minutes or until doubled in bulk.

Bake at 350° for 1 hour or until loaves sound hollow when tapped. Remove bread from pans immediately; cool on wire racks. Yield: 3 loaves.

MRS. YOHE'S ORIGINAL BROWN RICE BREAD

3 cups cooked brown rice
2 packages dry yeast
1 teaspoon sugar
¼ teaspoon ground ginger
2 cups warm water (105° to 115°), divided
¾ cup instant nonfat dry milk powder
¼ cup plus 2 tablespoons sugar
10 cups all-purpose flour, divided
¼ cup plus 2 tablespoons butter or margarine, softened
1 tablespoons salt

Cook rice according to package directions. Set aside, and cool to 105° to 115°.

Combine yeast, 1 teaspoon sugar, ginger, and ½ cup warm water; stir until yeast is dissolved. Set aside.

Combine 1½ cups warm water, milk powder, remaining sugar, and 4 cups flour; stir well. Stir in butter, salt, rice, 4 cups flour, and yeast mixture.

Turn dough out onto a surface sprinkled with remaining flour; knead 10 minutes or until smooth and elastic. Place in a greased bowl, turning to grease top. Cover and let rise in a warm place (85°), free from drafts, 1 hour or until doubled in bulk. Punch dough down; cover and let rest 10 minutes.

Divide dough into 4 equal portions, shaping each into a loaf. Place each loaf into a greased 8½- x 4½- x 3-inch loafpan. Cover; repeat rising procedure for 45 minutes or until doubled in bulk. Bake at 350° for 40 minutes or until loaves sound hollow when tapped. Remove bread from pans and cool on wire racks. Yield: 4 loaves.

Swedish Rye Bread (left), Mrs. Yohe's Original Brown Rice Bread, and Sunflower Seed Bread (front).

This Boy Has Not Been Trained to Eat Bread and Butter Properly

This Lad Breaks Off a Small Piece and Butters It Before Putting It in His Mouth

Lads, trained and untrained, à la "Standard Etiquette," 1925.

SWEDISH RYE BREAD

1 package dry yeast
½ cup warm water (105° to 115°)
2 cups sifted rye flour
¾ cup molasses
⅓ cup shortening
2 teaspoons salt
2 cups boiling water
6¾ cups all-purpose flour
1 egg, beaten

Dissolve yeast in warm water; let stand 5 minutes or until bubbly.

Combine rye flour, molasses, shortening, and salt; add boiling water, stirring until shortening is dissolved. Cool to 105° to 115°. Stir in dissolved yeast, and gradually add enough all-purpose flour to form a soft ball.

Turn dough out onto a floured surface; cover and let rest 10 minutes. Knead dough 10 minutes or until smooth and elastic. Shape into a ball, and place in a greased bowl; turning to grease top. Cover and let rise in a warm place (85°), free from drafts, 2 hours or until doubled in bulk. Punch dough down, and repeat rising procedure 30 minutes.

Turn dough out onto a lightly floured surface. Divide into 3 equal portions, shaping each portion into a smooth ball. Cover and let rest 15 minutes. Shape into round loaves, and place on greased baking sheets. Cover and repeat rising procedure 1 hour or until doubled in bulk. Brush loaves with egg. Bake at 350° for 40 minutes or until loaves sound hollow when tapped. Transfer loaves to wire racks to cool. Yield: 3 loaves.

SUNFLOWER SEED BREAD

2 packages dry yeast
2 cups warm water (105° to 115°)
⅔ cup sunflower seeds
½ cup honey
⅓ cup wheat bran
⅓ cup pumpkin seeds, finely chopped
2 tablespoons plus 2 teaspoons vegetable oil
2 teaspoons salt
6 to 7 cups whole wheat flour

Dissolve yeast in warm water in a large bowl, stirring well. Let stand 5 minutes or until bubbly. Add sunflower seeds, honey, bran, pumpkin seeds, oil, salt, and 4 cups flour; beat with a wooden spoon until smooth. Stir in enough remaining flour to make a soft dough.

Place dough in a greased bowl, turning to grease top. Cover and let rise in a warm place (85°), free from drafts, 1 hour or until doubled in bulk.

Punch dough down; shape into a ball. Return to greased bowl; cover and repeat rising procedure 45 minutes. Punch dough down, and turn out onto a lightly floured surface. Let rest 10 minutes.

Divide dough in half, shaping each into a loaf. Place in 2 greased 8½- x 4½- x 3-inch loafpans. Cover and repeat rising procedure 45 minutes. Bake at 350° for 35 minutes or until loaves sound hollow when tapped. Remove bread from pans immediately; cool on wire racks. Yield: 2 loaves.

ALL-OCCASION ROLLS

1 package dry yeast
1 tablespoon sugar, divided
1 cup warm milk (105° to 115°)
1 tablespoon shortening, melted
1 teaspoon salt
3 cups all-purpose flour, divided
Butter or margarine, melted (optional)

Dissolve yeast and 1 teaspoon sugar in warm milk in a large bowl, stirring well; let stand 5 minutes or until bubbly. Add remaining sugar, shortening, salt, and 1½ cups flour; beat at low speed of electric mixer until smooth. Stir in enough remaining flour to make a soft dough.

Place dough in a greased bowl, turning to grease top. Cover and let rise in a warm place (85°), free from drafts, 1 hour or until doubled in bulk.

Punch dough down, and let rest 5 minutes. Divide dough into 16 portions. Roll each portion into a 10-inch rope on a lightly floured surface. Loosely coil ropes on a greased baking sheet. Cover and repeat rising procedure 1 hour or until doubled in bulk. Bake at 350° for 15 minutes or until lightly browned. Brush rolls with melted butter, if desired. Yield: 16 rolls.

GENERALS

2 packages dry yeast
¼ cup plus 1½ teaspoons sugar, divided
3¼ cup warm water (105° to 115°), divided
9 cups all-purpose flour
1 tablespoon salt
3 tablespoons lard

Dissolve yeast and ½ teaspoon sugar in 1 cup warm water, stirring well. Let stand 5 minutes or until bubbly.

Sift together flour, remaining sugar, and salt in a large bowl. Cut in lard until mixture resembles coarse meal. Stir yeast mixture into flour mixture. Gradually stir in remaining warm water.

Turn dough out onto a lightly floured surface; knead 10 minutes or until smooth and elastic. Place dough in a greased bowl, turning to grease top. Cover and let rise in a warm place (85°), free from drafts, 1 hour and 20 minutes or until doubled in bulk. Punch dough down; turn out onto a floured surface. Cover and let rest 10 minutes.

Roll dough to ½-inch thickness; cut with a 2½-inch biscuit cutter. Place rolls on lightly greased baking sheets; cover and repeat rising procedure 45 minutes or until doubled in bulk. Bake at 450° for 10 minutes or until golden brown. Yield: about 4 dozen.

"These were my cousin General Washington's favourite breakfast cakes." We do wonder sometimes how recipes got their names; "Generals" appear to have been originated by a genuine kinswoman of Washington's. The recipe is a large one, and the cakes themselves are sizeable. One could make them smaller and call them "Lieutenants," but it would spoil the story.

National Gallery of Art

BUTTERMILK ROLLS

1 package dry yeast
2½ cups warm buttermilk (105° to 115°)
5 cups sifted all-purpose flour
¼ teaspoon baking powder
¼ teaspoon soda
3 tablespoons sugar
1 teaspoon salt
3 tablespoons lard
Butter or margarine, melted

Dissolve yeast in warm buttermilk; let stand 5 minutes or until bubbly. Set aside.

Sift together flour and remaining dry ingredients; cut in lard using a pastry blender until mixture resembles coarse meal.

Add yeast mixture, stirring until dry ingredients are moistened. Turn dough out onto a well-floured surface, and knead lightly 4 to 5 times.

Roll dough to ½-inch thickness; cut with a 2¼-inch biscuit cutter. Shape each roll into a round ball, and place ½ inch apart in two greased 9-inch round cakepans.

Cover; let rise in a warm place (85°), free from drafts, 1 hour or until doubled in bulk. Bake at 425° for 15 minutes or until lightly browned. Brush with butter. Yield: about 2½ dozen.

QUICK ROLLS

2 packages dry yeast
¼ cup warm water (105° to 115°)
1¼ cups milk
¼ cup lard
3 tablespoons sugar
¼ teaspoon salt
3 cups all-purpose flour

Dissolve yeast in warm water, stirring well. Let stand 5 minutes or until bubbly.

Combine milk, lard, sugar, and salt in a large heavy saucepan; heat to 105° to 115°. Stir in dissolved yeast and flour, mixing well. Cover and let rise in a warm place (85°), free from drafts, 15 minutes. Kneading is not necessary as dough is very soft and sticky.

Lightly grease muffin pans. With well-greased hands shape dough into 1-inch balls; place 3 balls in each muffin cup. Cover and repeat rising procedure 15 minutes. Bake at 450° for 8 minutes or until golden brown. Yield: 2 dozen.

RICH CRESCENT ROLLS

1 package dry yeast
½ cup sugar, divided
1 cup warm water (105° to 115°)
½ cup plus 1 tablespoon butter or margarine, melted
3 eggs, beaten
1 teaspoon salt
4½ cups all-purpose flour, divided

Combine yeast, 1 teaspoon sugar, and water; stir well. Let stand 5 minutes or until bubbly. Add remaining sugar, butter, eggs, salt, and 2¼ cups flour; beat at low speed of electric mixer 5 minutes or until smooth. Stir in enough remaining flour to make a soft dough.

Place dough in a greased bowl, turning to grease top. Cover and refrigerate overnight.

Punch dough down, and divide into four equal portions. Roll each portion into a circle 12 inches in diameter and ¼-inch thick; cut each circle into 12 wedges. Roll each wedge tightly, beginning at wide end.

Place rolls on greased baking sheets, point side down; curve into crescent shape. Cover and let rise in a warm place (85°), free from drafts, 1½ hours or until doubled in bulk. Bake at 450° for 8 minutes or until lightly browned. Yield: 4 dozen.

A pleasing effect is created in serving rolls in various shapes: Round Southern Rolls (top right), Crescent Rolls, and Quick Rolls in cloverleafs.

SOUTHERN ROLLS

1 package dry yeast
1 tablespoon sugar, divided
⅓ cup warm water (105°
   to 115°)
3 eggs, beaten
½ cup shortening, melted
⅓ cup warm milk (105°
   to 115°)
1 teaspoon salt
3¼ cups all-purpose flour
Butter or margarine,
   melted

Dissolve yeast and 1 teaspoon sugar in warm water; stir well. Let stand 5 minutes or until bubbly.

Combine remaining sugar, eggs, shortening, milk, and salt in a large mixing bowl; stir until sugar and salt are dissolved. Add yeast mixture, stirring well. Stir in enough flour to make a soft dough.

Place dough in a greased bowl, turning to grease top. Cover and let rise in a warm place (85°), free from drafts, 1 hour or until doubled in bulk. Punch dough down, and let rest 5 minutes.

Lightly grease muffin pans. Shape dough into 2-inch balls; place 1 ball in each muffin cup. Cover and repeat rising procedure 45 minutes or until doubled in bulk. Bake at 400° for 12 minutes or until lightly browned. Brush with melted butter. Yield: about 1½ dozen.

Our standards haven't changed much in generations of "light rolls," as Southerners like to call them. Is there any other kind? Possibly. Remember the yeast must be actively foaming before proceeding. When the recipe says, "knead," don't hold back. And realize that flour measurements are necessarily inexact; much depends on condition of flour, humidity, egg size, and so on. Use enough flour to keep dough from being sticky, then stop!

Inferior flours take flight when Payn's enters the kitchen.

LOUISIANA BULLFROGS

2 packages dry yeast
¼ cup sugar, divided
½ cup warm water (105°
  to 115°)
5½ cups all-purpose flour,
  divided
⅓ cup warm milk (105°
  to 115°)
6 eggs, well beaten
1 cup butter or margarine,
  melted
1½ teaspoons salt

Dissolve yeast and 1 teaspoon sugar in warm water, stirring well. Let stand 5 minutes or until bubbly.

Place 1 cup flour in a large mixing bowl; add yeast mixture, and stir well. Add warm milk, stirring until smooth. Turn dough out onto a lightly floured surface, and knead 5 minutes or until smooth and elastic. Place in a greased bowl, turning to grease top. Cover and let rise in a warm place (85°), free from drafts, 1 hour or until doubled in bulk.

Combine remaining sugar, eggs, and melted butter; add to dough, and stir well. Gradually add remaining flour and salt, stirring until well blended. Turn dough out onto a lightly floured surface, and knead 3 to 4 times. Cover and let rise in a warm place (85°), free from drafts, 1 hour or until doubled in bulk.

Divide dough into 12 equal portions. Shape each portion into a 3-inch square. Place squares in a greased 13- x 9- x 2-inch baking pan. Cover and repeat rising procedure 45 minutes or until doubled in bulk. Bake at 350° for 35 minutes or until lightly browned. Yield: 1 dozen.

ICE BOX ROLLS

1 package dry yeast
½ cup warm water (105° to
  115°)
2 cups milk
½ cup sugar
½ cup lard
5½ cups all-purpose flour
½ teaspoon baking powder
½ teaspoon baking soda
1 teaspoon salt

Dissolve yeast in warm water, stirring well. Let stand 5 minutes or until bubbly.

Scald milk; add sugar and lard, stirring well. Cool mixture to lukewarm (105° to 115°).

Add dissolved yeast to milk mixture; stir well. Add flour, baking powder, soda, and salt.

Turn dough out onto a floured surface; knead 8 minutes or until smooth. Place in a greased bowl, turning to grease top. Cover and let rise in a warm place (85°), free from drafts, 1 hour or until doubled in bulk.

Turn dough out onto a floured surface, and knead 3 to 4 times. Return dough to bowl; cover and chill until needed. (Dough may be stored in refrigerator several days.)

Divide dough into 48 portions. Roll each piece into a 10-inch rope, and tie into a loose knot, stretching rope gently if needed.

Place rolls on greased baking sheets. Cover and repeat rising procedure 30 minutes or until doubled in bulk. Bake at 450° for 8 minutes or until lightly browned. Yield: 4 dozen.

The ice box gave way to the refrigerator in the 1930s.

POTATO ICE BOX ROLLS

1 package dry yeast
½ cup sugar, divided
¼ cup warm water (105° to 115°)
2 cups milk, scalded
½ cup cooked, mashed potatoes
½ cup shortening, melted
1 teaspoon baking powder
1 teaspoon baking soda
1 teaspoon salt
6½ cups all-purpose flour, divided
Butter or margarine, melted (optional)

Combine yeast, 1 teaspoon sugar, and water in a large bowl; stir well. Let stand 5 minutes.

Combine remaining sugar, milk, potatoes, shortening, baking powder, soda, and salt; add to yeast mixture, stirring well. Stir in 2 cups flour. Cover and let rise in a warm place (85°), free from drafts, 1 hour or until doubled in bulk. Add enough remaining flour to make a soft dough.

Shape dough into a ball; place in a greased bowl, turning to grease top. Cover and refrigerate overnight.

Lightly grease muffin pans. Shape dough into 2-inch balls; place 1 ball in each muffin cup. Cover and let rise in a warm place (85°), free from drafts, 1 hour or until doubled in bulk. Using kitchen shears, cut a shallow cross on top of each roll. Bake at 400° for 10 minutes or until golden brown. Brush with melted butter, if desired. Yield: 2 dozen.

Potato Ice Box Rolls

SALLY LUNN MUFFINS

2 cups milk, scalded
1 cup shortening
2 packages dry yeast
3 eggs, beaten
¼ cup sugar
2 teaspoons salt
6 cups all-purpose flour
2 tablespoons butter or margarine, melted

Combine milk and shortening; stir until shortening melts. Let cool to 105° to 115°.

Add yeast, stirring until dissolved. Add eggs, sugar, and salt; beat well. Gradually add flour, stirring until smooth. Cover and let rise in a warm place (85°), free from drafts, 1 hour or until doubled in bulk.

Punch dough down; spoon into greased muffin pans, filling two-thirds full. Cover and repeat rising procedure 1 hour or until doubled in bulk. Bake at 350° for 18 minutes or until golden brown. Brush top of muffins with butter. Remove from pan; place on wire racks to cool. Yield: about 3½ dozen.

FOR SPECIAL OCCASIONS

1935 CHOCOLATE BREAD

1 package dry yeast
½ cup warm milk (105° to 115°)
2 cups sifted all-purpose flour, divided
3 tablespoons sugar
3 tablespoons cocoa
1 teaspoon salt
1 egg, beaten
1 teaspoon shortening, melted
1 cup chopped pecans
1 tablespoon vanilla extract
Vegetable oil

Dissolve yeast in warm milk; let stand 5 minutes.

Sift together 1½ cups flour, sugar, cocoa, and salt; set aside.

Combine dissolved yeast, egg, shortening, pecans, and vanilla; mix well. Gradually add flour mixture to make a soft dough.

Turn dough out onto a surface sprinkled with remaining ½ cup flour; knead 10 minutes or until smooth and elastic. Place in a well-greased bowl, turning to grease top. Cover and let rise in a warm place (85°), free from drafts, 1 hour or until doubled in bulk.

Punch dough down; turn out onto a floured surface, and shape into a loaf. Place in a greased 7½- x 3- x 2-inch loaf-pan. Brush top with oil; cover and repeat rising procedure 1 hour. Bake at 375° for 40 minutes or until loaf sounds hollow when tapped. Remove bread from pan immediately; cool on wire rack. Yield: 1 loaf.

CORNISH SAFFRON BREAD

1 package dry yeast
1½ teaspoons sugar
¾ cup warm water (105° to 115°)
5½ cups all-purpose flour, divided
¾ cup sugar
1½ teaspoons ground nutmeg
¾ teaspoon salt
¼ cup plus 2 tablespoons shortening
½ (4-ounce) package candied lemon peel, finely chopped
½ (4-ounce) package candied citron, finely chopped
1 cup currants
¾ cup raisins
½ cup chopped pecans
¼ teaspoon powdered saffron
¼ cup boiling water
½ cup milk
3 eggs, beaten

Dissolve yeast and 1½ teaspoons sugar in warm water, stirring well; let stand 5 minutes or until bubbly. Add 1 cup flour; mix well. Cover with plastic wrap, and let rise in a warm place (85°), free from drafts, 1 hour or until doubled in bulk.

Combine remaining flour, ¾ cup sugar, nutmeg, and salt in a large bowl; stir well. Cut in shortening until mixture resembles coarse meal. Add lemon peel, citron, currants, raisins, and pecans; stir well.

Dissolve saffron in boiling water; add milk, and cool to lukewarm (105° to 115°). Stir milk mixture and eggs into flour mixture. Add yeast mixture; mix well.

Spoon batter into 2 well-greased 8½- x 4½- x 3-inch loaf-pans. Cover and repeat rising procedure 1 hour. Bake at 350° for 50 minutes or until a wooden pick inserted in center comes out clean. Remove bread from pans, and cool on wire racks. Yield: 2 loaves.

1935 Chocolate Bread (left) and Cornish Saffron Bread.

GREEK HOLIDAY BREAD

5 whole bay leaves
2 cups boiling water
3 packages dry yeast
¼ cup warm water (105° to 115°)
2 cups sugar
1 cup butter or margarine, melted
5 eggs, beaten
1 cup milk
10 cups all-purpose flour, divided
1 egg, beaten
¼ cup milk
2 tablespoons sesame seeds

Combine bay leaves and boiling water; set aside to cool.

Dissolve yeast in warm water, stirring well; let stand 5 minutes or until bubbly.

Combine sugar, butter, and 5 eggs. Remove bay leaves from water; discard. Add seasoned water, 1 cup milk, and dissolved yeast to egg mixture, stirring well. Add 4 cups flour; beat well. Stir in enough remaining flour to make a soft dough. Cover; let rise in a warm place (85°), free from drafts, 3 hours or until doubled in bulk.

Punch dough down; turn out onto a floured surface. Divide into 6 equal portions, shaping each into a ball. Place each ball in a well-greased 8-inch round cakepan. Press down gently to fill pan. Cover loosely; repeat rising procedure 1½ hours or until doubled in bulk.

Combine egg and ¼ cup milk; stir well. Gently brush top of loaves with egg mixture; sprinkle 1 teaspoon sesame seeds over each loaf. Bake at 300° for 50 minutes or until golden brown. Cool 10 minutes on wire racks before removing from pans. Yield: 6 loaves.

SALZBURGER RAISIN BREAD

1½ cups milk
½ cup butter or margarine, softened
½ cup sugar
2 teaspoons salt
2 packages dry yeast
1 teaspoon sugar
1 cup warm water (105° to 115°)
2 eggs, beaten
7 to 8 cups all-purpose flour, divided
2½ cups raisins
¼ cup all-purpose flour
Butter or margarine, melted

Scald milk; remove from heat, and add butter, ½ cup sugar, and salt, stirring well. Let cool to lukewarm (105° to 115°).

Dissolve yeast and 1 teaspoon sugar in warm water; stir well, and let stand 5 minutes or until bubbly.

Combine cooled milk mixture and yeast mixture in a large bowl. Stir in eggs and 5 cups flour; mix well. Dredge raisins in ¼ cup flour, stirring to coat well; add to dough, stirring well.

Stir in enough remaining flour to form a firm dough. Turn out onto a lightly floured surface, and knead 7 to 8 times. Place in a greased bowl, turning to grease top. Cover and let rise in a warm place (85°), free from drafts, 1½ hours or until doubled in bulk.

Punch dough down; cover and let rest 10 minutes. Turn out onto a floured surface; divide dough into 3 equal portions, shaping each into a loaf. Place in 3 greased 8½- x 4½ x 3-inch loafpans. Cover and repeat rising procedure 45 minutes or until doubled in bulk.

Bake at 350° for 30 minutes or until loaves sound hollow when tapped. Remove bread from pans immediately, and cool on wire racks. Brush tops with butter. Yield: 3 loaves.

L ittle remains of the old Lutheran community of New Ebenezer, built in an area know as Effingham, about twenty-five miles from Savannah. Settled in 1734 by refugees fleeing religious persecution by the autocratic archbishops of Bavaria, the town was modeled after the town plan of Savannah. Once, briefly, New Ebenezer was the capital of Georgia.

The Salzburgers had come to Georgia at the invitation of General Oglethorpe, who met them when they landed in Charleston, then escorted them southward. Today, few reminders of their brave presence remain: the original church and cemetery, and a solitary house.

The influence of the immigrants is still felt in the community, however, and illustrates again the incredible diversity of our Southern foodways. One of their special-occasion breads is *kugelhof*, or *kogle loaf*, meaning raisin bread. Kogle, as many of the older generation in Effingham still call kugelhof, can be served with any meal. Traditionally baked in a turban-shaped kugelhof pan with a funnel in the center, it is no less delicious when baked in loaves.

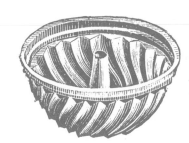

AMISH CAKES

1 package dry yeast
1 cup warm water (105°
  to 115°)
½ cup lard
½ cup sugar
3 eggs
1 teaspoon salt
5 cups all-purpose flour
1 cup firmly packed brown
  sugar
1 teaspoon ground cinnamon
¼ cup butter or margarine,
  softened
½ cup pecans, chopped

Dissolve yeast in warm water, stirring well. Let stand 5 minutes or until bubbly.

Cream lard; gradually add sugar, beating well. Add eggs, one at a time, beating well after each addition. Stir in dissolved yeast, salt, and enough flour to make a soft dough.

Place dough in a greased bowl, turning to grease top. Cover and let rise in a warm place (85°), free from drafts, 1 hour or until doubled in bulk. Punch dough down; cover and repeat rising procedure 1 hour.

Punch dough down. Divide dough into 3 equal portions, shaping each portion into a ball. Place each ball in a greased 9-inch piepan. Press lightly with fingertips to form a large bun. Cover and repeat rising procedure 1½ hours.

Combine brown sugar and cinnamon; cut in butter until mixture resembles coarse meal. Stir in pecans. Sprinkle mixture evenly over the buns. Bake at 350° for 30 minutes. Yield: three 9-inch coffee cakes.

1860 RAISIN COFFEE CAKE

2¾ to 3 cups all-purpose
  flour, divided
1½ tablespoons sugar
1 teaspoon salt
1 package dry yeast
1 cup water
2 tablespoons vegetable
  oil
¼ cup butter or margarine,
  melted
1 egg, beaten
¼ cup plus 2 tablespoons
  sugar
1 teaspoon ground
  cinnamon
½ cup raisins
1½ tablespoons candied
  orange peel, finely
  chopped
Powdered sugar glaze (recipe
  follows)

Combine 1 cup flour, 1½ tablespoons sugar, salt, and yeast in large mixing bowl. Heat water and oil to very warm (120° to 130°); add to flour mixture. Blend mixture at low speed of electric mixer until moistened. Beat 3 minutes at medium speed. Stir in enough remaining flour to make a stiff dough.

Turn dough out onto a lightly floured surface, and knead 8 minutes or until smooth and elastic. Place dough in a greased bowl, turning to grease top. Cover and let rise in a warm place (85°), free from drafts, 1 hour or until doubled in bulk.

Punch dough down; stir in butter, egg, ¼ cup plus 2 tablespoons sugar, cinnamon, raisins, and orange peel. Mix well. Spoon into a well-greased 6½-cup ring mold. Cover and repeat rising procedure 45 minutes. Bake at 350° for 25 to 30 minutes. Remove from mold; drizzle glaze over warm cake. Yield: one 9-inch coffee cake.

Powdered Sugar Glaze:

1 cup sifted powdered
  sugar
1 tablespoon milk
½ teaspoon vanilla extract

Combine all ingredients; mix well. Yield: about ½ cup.

OVERNIGHT KAFFEE KUCHEN

1 package dry yeast
2 tablespoons sugar
1½ cups warm water (105° to
  115°)
8 to 9 cups all-purpose flour,
  divided
½ cup sugar
½ cup milk
2 eggs, beaten
1 tablespoon butter or
  margarine, melted
1 teaspoon salt
1 cup raisins
Topping (recipe follows)

Dissolve yeast and 2 tablespoons sugar in warm water, stirring well. Let stand 5 minutes or until bubbly. Add 3 cups flour; beat well. Cover and let rise in a warm place (85°), free from drafts, overnight.

Add ½ cup sugar, milk, eggs, butter, salt, raisins, and enough remaining flour to make a stiff dough.

Shape dough into a ball; place in a greased bowl, turning to grease top. Cover and repeat rising procedure 1 hour or until doubled in bulk. Punch dough down and turn out onto a lightly floured surface. Knead 5 minutes or until smooth and elastic. Cover and let dough rest 10 minutes.

Divide dough in half. Roll each half into a 13- x 9-inch rectangle. Place in 2 greased 13- x 9- x 2-inch baking pans. Sprinkle topping evenly over the 2 coffee cakes. Cover and repeat rising procedure 1 hour or until doubled in bulk. Bake at 350° for 30 to 35 minutes. Yield: two 13- x 9-inch coffee cakes.

Topping:

½ cup all-purpose flour
½ cup sugar
1 teaspoon cinnamon
¼ cup butter or margarine
½ cup chopped pecans

Combine flour, sugar, and cinnamon; cut in butter with a pastry blender until mixture resembles coarse meal. Stir in pecans. Yield: about 1½ cups.
Note: Coffee cake freezes well.

MORAVIAN SUGAR CAKE

1 package dry yeast
½ teaspoon sugar
¼ cup warm water (105°
  to 115°)
1 cup hot mashed
  potatoes
1 cup sugar
½ cup shortening
¼ cup butter
1 teaspoon salt
2 eggs, beaten
3 cups all-purpose flour
1 cup butter, cut into
  ⅛-inch slices
1 cup firmly packed brown
  sugar
2 teaspoons ground
  cinnamon

Dissolve yeast and ½ teaspoon sugar in warm water; let stand 5 minutes or until bubbly.

Combine potatoes, 1 cup sugar, shortening, ¼ cup butter, and salt in a large mixing bowl; stir until shortening melts. Stir in yeast mixture.

Cover and let rise in a warm place (85°), free from drafts, 1½ hours or until spongy.

Stir in eggs and flour to make a soft dough. Shape dough into a ball. Place in a greased bowl, turning to grease top. Cover and repeat rising procedure 2 hours or until doubled in bulk.

Turn dough out onto a lightly floured surface; knead 5 minutes or until smooth and elastic. Divide dough in half; pat evenly into 2 greased 13- x 9- x 2-inch baking pans. Cover and repeat rising procedure 2 hours or until doubled in bulk.

Press slices of butter into dough in rows at ½-inch intervals. Top each slice of butter with 1 teaspoon brown sugar. Sprinkle 1 teaspoon cinnamon over each cake. Bake at 375° for 20 minutes or until golden brown. Yield: two 13- x 9-inch coffee cakes.

Courtesy of Old Salem, Inc.

Cutting Moravian sugar cake in Old Salem.

Winston-Salem's Moravian community has kept its Germanic bent for song and feast in a high state of polish through many generations. The tenets of their faith are straightforward: fellowship and brotherhood of God and man—proof again that good faith and fellowship go together. Famous for their baking over the centuries, the Moravians are well known for their Moravian Sugar Cake, probably the most widely disseminated of their recipes. Even more famous than Love Feast Buns? Or Christmas cookies almost thin enough to see right through? Coffee is the beverage of choice, and has been since the 1700s.

Prize-Winning Coffee Cake

HOT CROSS BUNS

1 cup milk
1 package dry yeast
1 tablespoon sugar
3¾ cups sifted all-purpose
    flour, divided
¼ cup butter or margarine,
    softened
⅓ cup sugar
1 egg
½ teaspoon salt
¼ cup raisins
1 egg, beaten
1 tablespoon water
1 cup powdered sugar
1 tablespoon milk

Scald milk; let cool to luke-warm (105° to 115°). Dissolve yeast and 1 tablespoon sugar in warm milk in a large mixing bowl, stirring well. Let stand 5 minutes or until bubbly.

Add 1¾ cups flour, mixing until smooth. Cover and let rise in a warm place (85°), free from drafts, 1½ hours or until doubled in bulk.

Cream butter; gradually add ⅓ cup sugar, beating well. Add egg and salt, mixing well. Stir in raisins, yeast mixture, and enough remaining flour to make a soft dough.

Turn dough out onto a floured surface. Knead 8 minutes or until smooth and elastic. Place dough in a greased bowl, turning to grease top. Cover and repeat rising procedure 1 hour or until doubled in bulk. Punch dough down. Turn out onto a lightly floured surface. Cover; let rest 10 minutes.

Divide dough into 18 pieces; shape into balls, and place 2 inches apart on greased baking sheets. Cover and repeat rising procedure 1 hour or until doubled in bulk.

Using a sharp knife, cut a shallow cross on top of each bun. Combine egg and water, stirring well; brush over each bun. Bake at 400° for 8 minutes or until golden brown; cool on wire racks.

Combine powdered sugar and 1 tablespoon milk; stir until smooth. Pipe icing into cross-shaped indentation on each bun. Yield: 1½ dozen.

PRIZE-WINNING COFFEE CAKE

1 package dry yeast
½ cup sugar, divided
¼ cup warm water (105° to
    115°)
½ cup butter or margarine,
    softened
1 teaspoon salt
2 eggs, beaten
1 cup milk
1 tablespoon lemon juice
¼ teaspoon ground nutmeg
4½ cups all-purpose flour
Topping (recipe follows)
Glaze (recipe follows)

Dissolve yeast and 1 teaspoon sugar in warm water, stirring well. Let stand 5 minutes or until bubbly.

Cream butter; gradually add remaining sugar and salt, beating until light and fluffy. Add eggs, milk, lemon juice, and nutmeg; beat well. Stir in yeast mixture. Add flour; beat until smooth.

Turn dough out onto a floured surface, and knead 5 minutes. Place in a greased bowl, turning to grease top. Let rise in a warm place (85°), free from drafts, 2 hours or until doubled in bulk.

Punch dough down; turn out onto a lightly floured surface. Divide dough in half. Roll each portion into a 1-inch diameter rope. Shape each rope into a loose coil in 2 greased 9-inch round cakepans, beginning at outer edge of pan. Firmly pinch ends to seal.

Spread half of topping over each cake. Cover and repeat rising procedure 45 minutes or until doubled in bulk. Bake at 350° for 30 minutes or until golden brown. Place on wire racks to cool. While cakes are warm, drizzle with glaze. Yield: two 9-inch coffee cakes.

Topping:

⅔ cup sifted powdered sugar
¼ cup butter or margarine,
    melted
2 tablespoons honey
1 egg white

Combine all ingredients, stirring until smooth. Yield: about ¾ cup.

Glaze:

2 cups sifted powdered sugar
3 tablespoons boiling water
1 teaspoon vanilla extract

Combine all ingredients, and beat until smooth. Yield: about 1 cup.

PAN DULCE

1 cup water
1 tablespoon anise seeds
2 packages dry yeast
6 cups all-purpose flour
2 teaspoons ground
  cinnamon
¼ teaspoon salt
¾ cup sugar
6 eggs
⅓ cup shortening, softened
Butter or margarine, melted
Sweet Bun Topping

Combine water and anise in a small saucepan; bring to a boil. Cook until mixture is reduced to ¾ cup. Strain mixture, reserving liquid and 1½ teaspoons anise seeds. Let cool to lukewarm (105° to 115°). Add yeast, and stir until dissolved. Let stand 20 minutes.

Sift together flour, cinnamon, and salt; set aside. Combine yeast mixture, sugar, and 2 cups sifted dry ingredients in a large mixing bowl, beating well. Add eggs, one at a time, beating well after each addition. Add shortening; beat at high speed of electric mixer until smooth. Stir in remaining dry ingredients to make a soft dough. (Dough will be very sticky.) Cover and let rise in a warm place (85°), free from drafts, 1 hour or until doubled in bulk.

Grease hands. Turn dough out onto a heavily floured surface, and knead 8 minutes or until smooth and elastic.

Divide dough into 30 pieces; shape into balls, and place 2 inches apart on greased baking sheets. Brush each bun with melted butter, and sprinkle heavily with Sweet Bun Topping. Cover and repeat rising procedure 1 hour or until doubled in bulk. Bake at 350° for 10 minutes or until golden brown. Yield: 2½ dozen.

Inventive flour advertisement has a story to tell.

Sweet Bun Topping:
¼ cup plus 2 tablespoons
  sifted powdered sugar
2 tablespoons cocoa
2 tablespoons all-purpose
  flour
3 tablespoons butter or
  margarine

Combine powdered sugar, cocoa, and flour; cut in butter with a pastry blender until mixture resembles coarse meal. Place in freezer for 30 minutes; transfer mixture to refrigerator until ready to use. Yield: about ½ cup.

SOUTHERN KITCHEN CINNAMON ROLLS

2 packages dry yeast
1 teaspoon sugar
¼ cup warm water (105° to 115°)
1 cup milk, scalded
1 cup butter or margarine
⅔ cup sugar
2 eggs, beaten
1 teaspoon salt
5 cups all-purpose flour
¾ cup butter or margarine, melted
2 cups sugar
1 cup firmly packed brown sugar
2 tablespoons cinnamon

Combine yeast, 1 teaspoon sugar, and warm water; stir well, and let stand 5 minutes or until bubbly.

Combine milk and butter in a large bowl, stirring until butter melts. Add ⅔ cup sugar, eggs, and salt, stirring well. Stir in yeast mixture and enough flour to make a soft dough. Place in a greased bowl, turning to grease top. Cover and let rise in a warm place (85°), free from drafts, 1 hour or until doubled in bulk.

Turn dough out onto a lightly floured surface; divide in half. Roll each half into a 20- x 8-inch rectangle; brush with melted butter, leaving a 1-inch margin on all sides. Combine 2 cups sugar, brown sugar, and cinnamon; sprinkle evenly over each rectangle of dough.

Roll each half up jellyroll fashion, beginning at long side; moisten edges with water to seal. Cut rolls into 1-inch slices; place slices, cut side down, in a greased 15- x 10- x 1-inch jellyroll pan. Cover and repeat rising procedure 1 hour or until doubled in bulk. Bake at 375° for 20 minutes or until lightly browned. Yield: about 3½ dozen.

Portrait of Nellie Custis Lewis by Charles Peale Polk, c.1810.

NELLIE CUSTIS LEWIS'S PHILADELPHIA BUNS

⅔ cup milk
½ cup butter or margarine
4 cups all-purpose flour, divided
½ cup sugar
2 packages dry yeast
1 teaspoon salt
½ teaspoon ground cinnamon
2 eggs, beaten
1 cup currants
1 egg white, slightly beaten
2 cups sifted powdered sugar
¼ cup milk

Combine ⅔ cup milk and butter in a saucepan; heat to 130°. Set aside.

Combine 2 cups flour, sugar, yeast, salt, and cinnamon in a large bowl; add milk mixture, and beat 5 minutes at medium speed of electric mixer. Add eggs, and stir well. Fold in currants and enough remaining flour to make a soft dough.

Turn dough out onto a floured surface; knead 4 to 6 minutes or until smooth and elastic. Place dough in a greased bowl, turning to grease top. Cover and let rise in a warm place (85°), free from drafts, 1 hour or until doubled in bulk.

Punch dough down, and let rest 5 minutes. Turn out onto a floured surface, and roll to ½-inch thickness; cut with a 2-inch biscuit cutter. Place buns on lightly greased baking sheets. Cover and repeat rising procedure 1 hour or until doubled in bulk. Brush buns with egg white. Bake at 350° for 15 minutes or until lightly browned. Cool on wire racks. Combine powdered sugar and ¼ cup milk; mix well. Drizzle over warm buns. Yield: 2 dozen.

ANNA MAUDE'S HONEY ALMOND ROLLS

2 packages dry yeast
1⅓ cups plus 1 teaspoon sugar, divided
2½ cups warm water (105° to 115°)
3 eggs, beaten
½ cup shortening, melted
¼ cup nonfat-dry milk powder
1 tablespoon salt
9½ cups all-purpose flour, divided
1 cup butter or margarine, softened
1 cup honey, divided
3 (2½-ounce) packages sliced almonds, toasted and divided
4 cups sifted powdered sugar
¼ cup plus 2 tablespoons water

Dissolve yeast and 1 teaspoon sugar in warm water in a large mixing bowl, stirring well; let stand 5 minutes or until bubbly. Add ⅓ cup sugar, eggs, shortening, milk powder, salt, and 4¾ cups flour; beat at low speed of electric mixer until smooth. Stir in enough remaining flour to make a soft dough (dough will be sticky).

Place dough in a greased bowl, turning to grease top. Cover and let rise in a warm place (85°), free from drafts, 1 hour or until doubled in bulk.

Cream butter; gradually add remaining 1 cup sugar, beating until light and fluffy. Add ¾ cup honey, beating well. Set aside.

Punch dough down; let rest 5 minutes. Turn dough out onto a floured surface; divide dough in half. Roll each half into a 12- x 8-inch rectangle, and spread each with half of butter-honey mixture. Sprinkle one-third of

Anna Maude's Honey Almond Rolls, terrific with tea.

toasted almonds over each rectangle. Roll up jellyroll fashion, beginning at long side; moisten edges with water to seal. Cut rolls in 1-inch slices; place slices, cut side down, in two 13- x 9- x 2-inch baking pans.

Bake at 350° for 25 minutes or until lightly browned. Combine powdered sugar, water, and remaining honey, mixing well; drizzle over warm rolls, and sprinkle with remaining almonds. Yield: 3 dozen.

KOLACHES

1 package dry yeast
¼ cup plus 1 tablespoon sugar, divided
½ cup warm water (105° to 115°)
7 cups all-purpose flour, divided
1 cup milk
¾ cup butter or margarine, melted
1 egg, beaten
1 teaspoon salt
Filling variations (recipes follow)

Dissolve yeast and 1 tablespoon sugar in warm water in a large bowl. Add 1 cup flour; stir well. Cover; let rise in a warm place (85°), free from drafts, 1 hour or until doubled in bulk.

Scald milk; cool to lukewarm (105° to 115°). Stir yeast sponge down; add remaining sugar, milk, butter, egg, and salt; stir well. Add enough remaining flour to make a soft dough. Cover; repeat rising procedure 1 hour or until doubled in bulk.

Punch dough down, and let rest 5 minutes. Turn out onto a floured surface, and roll to ½-inch thickness; cut with a 2½-inch biscuit cutter.

Make an indentation in the center of each roll using thumb; fill indentation with 1 teaspoon of desired filling.

Cover and repeat rising procedure 45 minutes or until doubled in bulk. Bake at 400° for 12 minutes or until lightly browned. Yield: about 2 dozen.

Pineapple Filling:

1 (8-ounce) can crushed pineapple, undrained
1 cup sugar
2 tablespoons all-purpose flour
2 tablespoons butter or margarine

Bring pineapple to a boil in a medium saucepan; add sugar and flour, stirring well. Cook over low heat 5 minutes or until sauce thickens. Remove from heat, and add butter; stir until butter melts. Yield: 1 cup.

Prune Filling:

1 cup dried prunes, chopped
⅓ cup water
½ cup sugar
1 tablespoon butter or margarine, melted
½ teaspoon vanilla extract

Combine first 3 ingredients in a saucepan; stir. Cover; cook over medium heat until liquid is absorbed and prunes are tender. Remove from heat. Stir in butter and vanilla. Yield: ¾ cup.

Apricot Filling:

1 cup dried apricots, chopped
½ cup water
½ cup sugar
1 tablespoon butter or margarine, melted
¼ teaspoon almond extract

Combine first 3 ingredients in a saucepan; stir well. Cover; cook over medium heat until liquid is absorbed and apricots are tender. Remove from heat. Stir in butter and extract. Yield: about ¾ cup.

Breads for special occasions deserve the finest ingredients.

Limoges china with an orange fruit and leaf pattern was the wedding gift of the Henry Morrison Flaglers to his secretary.

ORANGE ROLLS

2 packages dry yeast
⅓ cup sugar, divided
1 cup warm milk (105° to 115°)
3 eggs, beaten
¼ cup shortening, melted
1 teaspoon salt
2 teaspoons grated orange rind
4 cups all-purpose flour
¼ cup firmly packed brown sugar, divided

Dissolve yeast and 1 teaspoon sugar in warm milk; stir well, and let stand 5 minutes or until bubbly.

Combine remaining sugar, eggs, shortening, salt, orange rind, and yeast mixture, stirring well. Add enough flour to make a soft dough. Turn dough out onto a floured surface, and knead 8 minutes or until smooth and elastic.

Place dough in a greased bowl, turning to grease top. Cover and let rise in a warm place (85°), free from drafts, 1 hour or until doubled in bulk.

Punch dough down, and let rest 5 minutes. Lightly grease muffin pans, and place ½ tea-spoon brown sugar in bottom of each muffin cup. Shape dough into 2-inch balls; place 1 ball in each muffin cup. Cover and re-peat rising procedure 1 hour or until doubled in bulk.

Bake at 375° for 10 minutes or until golden brown.
Yield: 2 dozen.

SWEET ROLLS IN NEW DRESS

1 package dry yeast
1 cup sugar, divided
½ cup warm water (105° to 115°)
1 teaspoon salt
¾ cup butter or margarine, softened
1 cup milk
3 eggs, beaten
1 cup cooked, mashed potatoes
6 cups all-purpose flour, divided
1 cup apricot marmalade
Glaze (recipe follows)

Combine yeast, 1 teaspoon sugar, and warm water in a mix-ing bowl; stir well, and let stand 5 minutes or until bubbly. Add salt, butter, milk, eggs, pota-toes, and 1 cup flour; mix well. Cover and let rise in a warm place (85°), free from drafts, 2 hours or until doubled in bulk.

Stir mixture well; add remain-ing flour, mixing well. Turn dough out onto a lightly floured surface, and knead 5 minutes or until smooth and elastic. Let rest 5 minutes.

Roll dough to ½-inch thick-ness on a lightly floured surface; cut with a 2-inch biscuit cutter. Place about ½ inch apart in four greased 13- x 9- x 2-inch baking pans. Cover and repeat rising procedure 2 hours or until dou-bled in bulk.

Make an indentation in top of each roll with thumb. Spoon 1 teaspoon apricot marmalade into each indentation. Bake at 350° for 20 minutes or until golden brown. Remove rolls from pans; cool on wire racks. Drizzle glaze over tops of warm rolls. Yield: about 4 dozen.

Glaze:

1 cup sifted powdered sugar
2 tablespoons milk
½ teaspoon vanilla extract

Combine all ingredients; mix well. Yield: about ½ cup.

HERREN'S SWEET ROLLS

1 cup milk, scalded
¼ cup butter or margarine
¼ cup sugar, divided
1¼ teaspoons salt
2 packages dry yeast
¼ cup warm water (105° to
   115°)
4 cups sifted all-purpose flour
¼ cup butter or margarine,
   melted
1½ cups sugar
¼ cup ground cinnamon
2 tablespoons butter or
   margarine, melted

Combine milk, ¼ cup butter, 3 tablespoons plus 2 teaspoons sugar, and salt; stir until butter melts. Cool mixture to lukewarm (105° to 115°).

Combine yeast, remaining 1 teaspoon sugar, and warm water; stir well, and let stand 5 minutes or until bubbly. Add to cooled milk mixture, stirring well. Gradually add flour, stirring well.

Turn dough out onto a lightly floured surface; cover and let rest 15 minutes. Knead 5 minutes or until smooth and elastic. Place dough in a greased bowl, turning to grease top. Cover and let rise in a warm place (85°), free from drafts, 1½ hours or until doubled in bulk.

Turn dough out onto a floured surface; roll into a 16- x 8-inch rectangle. Cut into two 8-inch squares. Brush ¼ cup melted butter over dough. Combine 1½ cups sugar and cinnamon; stir well. Sprinkle 2 tablespoons of sugar-cinnamon mixture over each square. Roll up jellyroll fashion; continue rolling until each roll is about 15 inches in length. Moisten edges with water to seal. Cut rolls into ½-inch slices.

Sprinkle 1 cup of sugar-cinnamon mixture in the bottom of 2 well-greased 8-inch square baking pans. Place rolls, cut side down and ½-inch apart, over sugar mixture. Brush tops of rolls with 2 tablespoons melted butter, and sprinkle with remaining sugar-cinnamon mixture. Using a fork, gently lift center of rolls to form a peak.

Cover and repeat rising procedure 1½ hours. Bake at 350° for 25 minutes or until lightly browned. Yield: about 3 dozen.

Boca Raton Pecan Rolls (front) and Pecan Twists.

BOCA RATON PECAN ROLLS

1½ cups butter or margarine,
  softened
5½ cups bread flour, divided
2 eggs
2 packages dry yeast
1 teaspoon sugar
1 cup warm milk (105° to
  115°)
½ cup sugar
½ cup butter or margarine,
  melted
3 eggs, beaten
½ teaspoon salt
¼ cup butter or margarine,
  softened
2 cups firmly packed brown
  sugar
2 tablespoons honey
1 tablespoon water
1 tablespoon vegetable oil
1 cup chopped pecans
½ cup butter or margarine,
  melted
¼ cup sugar
1 teaspoon ground
  cinnamon

Cream butter; gradually add
½ cup flour, beating well. Add 2
eggs, one at a time, beating well
after each addition. Place waxed
paper on a large wet baking
sheet. Spread butter mixture
evenly into an 11- x 7-inch rectangle on the waxed paper, and
chill well.

Dissolve yeast and 1 teaspoon
sugar in milk in a large bowl;
stir well. Let stand 5 minutes or
until bubbly. Add ½ cup sugar,
½ cup melted butter, 3 eggs,
salt, and 3 cups flour; beat at
low speed of electric mixer until
smooth. Stir in enough remaining flour to make a soft dough.
Cover; chill 30 minutes.

Roll dough into a 16- x 12-
inch rectangle. Fit chilled butter
mixture over half of dough leaving a margin at the edges; remove waxed paper. Fold dough
over butter; pinch edges to seal.

Place folded edge of dough to
the right; roll dough to a 16- x
8-inch rectangle. (If butter
breaks through dough, flour
heavily, and continue rolling.)
Fold rectangle into thirds; pinch
edges to seal. Wrap dough in
waxed paper; chill 1 hour. Re-

Historic Cathedral Dining Room, Boca Raton Hotel and Club.

peat rolling, folding, and sealing
process; chill 30 minutes. Repeat rolling, folding, and sealing
process again; wrap dough in
foil, and refrigerate overnight.

Cream ¼ cup butter; gradually add brown sugar, honey,
water, and oil, beating well. Stir
in pecans. Sprinkle sugar mixture evenly into two 15- x 10- x
1-inch jellyroll pans.

Roll chilled dough into a 16- x
8-inch rectangle; brush with remaining ½ cup butter. Leave a
narrow margin on all sides.

Combine ¼ cup sugar and
cinnamon; sprinkle evenly over
dough. Roll up jellyroll fashion,
beginning at long side; moisten
edges with water to seal. Cut
rolls into ¾-inch slices; place
slices, cut side down, in prepared jellyroll pans. Cover and
let rise in a warm place, free
from drafts, 1 hour or until doubled in bulk. Bake at 375° for 12
minutes or until lightly
browned. Invert rolls immediately onto a cookie sheet. Yield:
about 2 dozen.

PECAN TWISTS

2 packages dry yeast
½ cup warm milk (105° to
  115°)
1 tablespoon sugar
3 cups sifted all-purpose
  flour, divided
1½ teaspoons salt
½ cup butter or margarine
2 eggs, beaten
1 teaspoon vanilla extract
¾ cup sugar
¾ cup chopped pecans

Combine yeast, milk, and 1
tablespoon sugar in a large
bowl; stir well. Let stand 5 minutes or until bubbly.

Combine 1½ cups flour and
salt; stir well. Cut in butter with
a pastry blender until mixture
resembles coarse meal. Gradually add flour mixture, mixing

well. Cover and let rise in a
warm place (85°), free from
drafts, 20 minutes.

Add eggs, vanilla, and remaining flour; stir well. (Dough will
be slightly sticky.) Tie dough
loosely in a large piece of cheesecloth; drop into a deep pan of
cool water (70° to 80°). Let stand
1 hour or until dough rises to
top of water. Remove from
water. Remove cheesecloth, and
shape dough into 1½-inch balls.

Combine sugar and pecans;
roll each ball in sugar mixture.
Twist dough into figure 8
shapes, and place on greased
baking sheets. Let stand 5 minutes. Bake at 400° for 12 minutes or until lightly browned.
Yield: about 3 dozen.

THE SOUTHERN FAVORITE

It sometimes happens that a visitor to Southern climes meets with a surprise at biscuit time. He has heard about biscuits; he knows that they're fluffy and brown and come in relays from the oven. Then, unwarned, he is served beaten biscuits at a party, and each bite sends a cascade of crumbs down the front of his shirt. Now really, you all. We should lead the innocent gently to his first sampling, lest he become hostile and adopt the attitude of Eliza Leslie, the Philadelphia savant who, in the 1850s, dismissed beaten biscuits as fit to eat only if one had nothing else.

"Beat 500 times for company, 300 times for family. . ." Small wonder beaten biscuits are seen less often in our generation. Not that Southerners got tired of eating them; people understandably wearied of making them. Happily, some hostesses still consider them a must, especially with slivers of country ham.

Much as a Southerner loves his cornbread, and as prideful as he is about his yeast baking, he reserves a special place in his heart for biscuits made with baking powder or buttermilk. Whereas commercial yeast and its wild cousin, sourdough, are slow to act, biscuits and other quick breads made with chemical leavening can be mixed while the oven is heating and popped right in to bake.

The texture, cellular structure, and flavor of chemically leavened breads are quite different from those of yeast products. Sometimes we combine the two leavens to make yeast biscuits, or, as they say in Southern Kentucky, "Riz Biscuits." Buttermilk biscuits, sweetened with soda came first. When baking powder finally made its appearance in the 1850s, it was really the same pair of ingredients cooks had been juggling for years to form carbon dioxide, the leavening gas: sodium bicarbonate and phosphate salt. But now it was in the right proportions, with starch added to keep the particles separated. Light, airy biscuits instantly mustered an army of admirers. Soon many cooks were serving both cornbread and biscuits with nearly every meal.

The plump, tender biscuit is the Queen Mother of a large family of goodies. We can make a basic dough into a partified sweet or glorify it with nuts, fruits, or benne seeds, as the notion strikes us. We give you the sublime biscuit.

Colorful old soda advertisement gives a clue to soda-buttermilk leavening in this batch of Southern biscuits: (clockwise from top) Cathead Biscuits (page 85), Virginia Buttermilk Biscuits (page 85), Bran Biscuits (page 89).

THE BEATEN BISCUIT

BEATEN BISCUITS

4 cups all-purpose flour
1 teaspoon salt
1 cup shortening
¾ cup ice water

Combine flour and salt; stir well. Cut in shortening until mixture resembles coarse meal. Sprinkle ice water evenly over flour mixture, stirring until dry ingredients are moistened.

Turn dough out onto a lightly floured surface. Beat dough with a rolling pin or wooden mallet for 20 minutes or until blisters appear, folding the dough over frequently.

Roll dough to ¼-inch thickness; cut with a 1¾-inch biscuit cutter. Prick biscuits with fork tines; place on ungreased baking sheets. Bake at 500° for 12 minutes or until lightly browned. Yield: 4½ dozen.

"BREAD BRAKE" BISCUITS

½ cup cold water
½ cup cold milk
4 cups all-purpose flour
1 tablespoon sugar
1 teaspoon baking powder
1 teaspoon salt
¼ cup shortening
¼ cup butter or margarine, melted

Combine water and milk; stir well, and chill thoroughly.

Combine flour, baking powder, sugar, and salt; stir well. Cut in shortening using a pastry blender until mixture resembles coarse meal. Add milk mixture, and stir with a fork until dry ingredients are moistened. Shape dough into a ball, and chill.

Press chilled dough through a bread brake until air bubbles form. Repeat procedure for 30 minutes, folding dough each time to incorporate air between the layers.

Roll dough to ½-inch thickness; cut with a 1¾-inch biscuit cutter. Place biscuits on lightly greased baking sheets. Prick biscuits with the tines of a fork, and brush with melted butter. Bake at 350° for 30 minutes. Yield: about 2 dozen.

The late nineteenth century saw vegetable shortening claiming a place in the market. Lard and butter had to make room. In this ad, elves man an early projector to "push" Cottolene. Refined cotton seed oil and shortening opened new markets for cotton farmers.

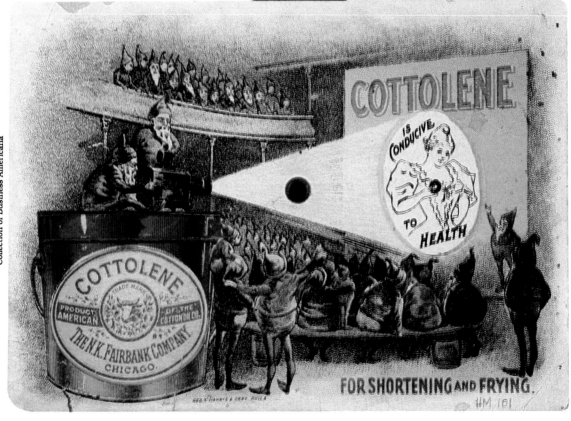

Collection of Business Americana

KENTUCKY BEATEN BISCUITS

3 cups all-purpose flour
1 teaspoon baking powder
1 tablespoon sugar
1 teaspoon salt
2 tablespoons lard, softened
½ cup milk
½ cup water

Combine flour, baking powder, sugar, and salt; stir well. Cut in lard until mixture resembles coarse meal. Sprinkle milk and water evenly over flour mixture, stirring until dry ingredients are moistened.

Turn dough out onto a lightly floured surface. Beat with a rolling pin or wooden mallet for 30 minutes or until blisters appear, folding dough over frequently.

Roll dough to ¼-inch thickness; cut with a 1¾-inch biscuit cutter. Prick biscuits with the tines of a fork. Place biscuits on greased baking sheets. Bake at 350° for 45 minutes or until lightly browned. Yield: 3 dozen.

MARYLAND BEATEN BISCUITS

7 cups all-purpose flour
½ teaspoon baking powder
1½ teaspoons sugar
1½ teaspoons salt
¾ cup lard
2½ cups ice water

Combine flour, baking powder, sugar, and salt; stir well. Cut in lard with a pastry blender until mixture resembles coarse meal. Sprinkle ice water evenly over flour mixture, stirring until dry ingredients are moistened.

Turn dough out onto a lightly floured surface. Beat with a rolling pin or mallet for 30 minutes or until blisters appear, folding dough over frequently.

Shape dough into 1-inch balls; flatten and prick with the tines of a fork. Place biscuits on ungreased baking sheets. Bake at 500° for 20 minutes or until lightly browned. Yield: about 3 dozen.

Most Southerners still making beaten biscuits today have a biscuit brake, now an antique, mounted on a marble slab and fitted either with a crank handle or with electrically driven belts. The dough is fed through the rollers exactly like wet clothes through an old-fashioned wringer. The dough is folded, then fed through again and again until it "snaps" and blisters. This folding is the secret of flakiness because of air entrapped with every fold. The layers of air-fat-flour make the biscuit split cleanly when served. For this reason, beaten biscuits made with the food processor may be less than perfect; although they taste right, there are no flaky layers. A fair compromise is to put the dough

Biscuit brake in original kitchen, Shirley Plantation.

through the coarse blade of a regular food grinder, folding and feeding the strings of dough through over and over.

Standard 1½-inch beaten biscuit cutters are made with six prongs attached inside which pierce the dough as the biscuit is cut. If one is not available to you, use a sharp three-tined "granny fork" and make two rows of holes in the center. The baked biscuit is popped open from the side with a knife tip or fork tine; they are never to be broken by hand or sliced through.

PROCESSOR BEATEN BISCUITS

2½ cups all-purpose flour
½ cup shortening
½ teaspoon baking powder
½ teaspoon salt
½ cup plus 1 tablespoon ice water

Position knife blade in processor bowl. Add flour, shortening, baking powder, and salt; cover. Process 5 seconds or until mixture resembles coarse meal.

With processor running, add ice water in a steady stream through food chute until dough forms a ball. Process dough an additional 2 minutes.

Roll dough out onto a lightly floured surface to ¼-inch thickness. Cut with a 1½-inch biscuit cutter. (Cut efficiently, for leftover dough should not be re-rolled.) Prick tops of biscuits with the tines of a fork.

Place on ungreased baking sheets. Bake at 400° for 20 minutes or until biscuits are lightly browned. Yield: about 4½ dozen.

BEATEN BISCUIT HOW-TO

Step 1—To make traditional beaten biscuits, first you need a biscuit brake. Press dough through the biscuit brake, turning handle rapidly to pull dough through rollers.

Step 2—Fold dough in half; press through rollers. Repeat procedure for 30 minutes or until dough begins to pop.

Step 4—Transfer biscuits to a lightly greased baking sheet. Prick through entire thickness of each biscuit several times with the tines of a fork.

Step 5—Coat the surface of each beaten biscuit with melted butter. Bake according to recipe directions.

Step 3—Place dough on a lightly floured surface. Using a small biscuit cutter, cut out biscuits efficiently. Remaining dough should be discarded as biscuits become tough when dough is rerolled.

Beaten biscuits were a breakfast specialty in the Deep South before the Civil War. They were also served as a classic accompaniment to Virginia ham.

Cooking for a cattle drive or a roundup in pioneeer Texas was not for the faint of heart. The cook could be lame. He could be cantankerous, even a part-time drunkard. But all was forgiven if he could turn out the trail driver's dream, sourdough biscuits, hot, brown, and yeasty-flavored. Keeping his starter alive and working was the cook's first duty, even if he had to sleep with the keg in his bedroll on cold nights. He baked his biscuits in a Dutch oven with coals on the lid to brown the tops.

Oversized Chuck Wagon Biscuits for man-sized appetites.

ANGEL BISCUITS

1 package dry yeast
½ cup warm water (105° to 115°)
5 cups self-rising flour
¾ cup shortening
1 teaspoon baking soda
2 cups buttermilk
3 tablespoons sugar

Combine yeast and warm water, stirring to dissolve; let stand 5 minutes or until bubbly. Set aside.

Place flour in a large bowl; cut in shortening with a pastry blender until mixture resembles coarse meal. Dissolve soda in buttermilk; add to flour mixture, stirring with a fork. Stir in sugar and yeast mixture, mixing well. Cover tightly and refrigerate 8 hours or overnight.

Turn dough out onto a lightly floured surface, and knead 4 to 5 times.

Roll dough to ½-inch thickness; cut with a 2-inch biscuit cutter. Place biscuits on greased baking sheets. Cover and let rise 1 hour. Bake at 400° for 12 minutes or until lightly browned. Yield: about 4 dozen.

CHUCK WAGON BISCUITS

2 packages dry yeast
1 cup warm water (105° to 115°)
2 cups buttermilk
¾ cup vegetable oil
7 cups all-purpose flour
3 tablespoons baking powder
½ teaspoon baking soda
¼ cup sugar
1½ teaspoons salt

Combine yeast and warm water in a small mixing bowl, stirring to dissolve; let stand 5 minutes or until bubbly. Add buttermilk and oil to yeast mixture; stir well.

Combine dry ingredients in a large bowl. Add buttermilk mixture, stirring with a fork until dry ingredients are moistened.

Turn dough out onto a floured surface, and knead 3 to 4 times.

Shape dough into 2-inch balls; place ⅛-inch apart in three well-greased 9-inch cast-iron skillets. Cover and let rise in a warm place (85°), free from drafts, 1½ hours or until doubled in bulk. Bake at 425° for 12 minutes or until golden brown. Yield: 3 dozen.

Note: Biscuits may be placed in greased baking pans to rise and bake.

SOURDOUGH BISCUITS

3 cups all-purpose flour
1 tablespoon baking
  powder
1 tablespoon sugar
¾ teaspoon salt
2 tablespoons shortening
2½ cups prepared Sourdough
  Starter (at room
  temperature)
3 tablespoons butter or
  margarine, melted

Combine flour, baking powder, sugar, and salt; stir well. Cut in shortening until mixture resembles coarse meal. Add Sourdough Starter; stir until moistened. Turn dough out onto a lightly floured surface, and knead 10 to 12 times.

Shape dough into 1½-inch balls, and place in a well-greased 13- x 9- x 2-inch baking pan.

Brush tops of biscuits with melted butter. Cover and let rise 1 hour and 45 minutes or until doubled in bulk. Bake at 400° for 20 minutes or until golden brown. Yield: 2 dozen.

Sourdough Starter:

1 package dry yeast
2 cups warm water (105° to
  115°)
2 cups all-purpose flour
1 tablespoon sugar

Dissolve yeast in warm water; let stand 5 minutes. Combine flour and sugar in a medium-size nonmetal bowl; mix well. Gradually stir in yeast mixture. Cover loosely wih plastic wrap or cheesecloth, and let stand in a warm place (80° to 85°) for 10 to 12 hours. Yield: about 2½ cups.

Left: Biscuits coming up. Below: Men of the LS Ranch, Texas, 1908.

TOPKNOT BISCUITS

1 package dry yeast
¼ cup warm water (105°
  to 115°)
2 cups all-purpose flour
2 teaspoons baking powder
2 teaspoons sugar
1 teaspoon salt
3 tablespoons shortening
¾ cup milk
Melted butter or margarine

Combine yeast and warm water, stirring to dissolve; let stand 5 minutes or until bubbly. Set aside.

Sift together dry ingredients. Cut in shortening with a pastry blender until mixture resembles coarse meal; add yeast mixture and milk, and mix well. Turn dough out onto a floured surface; knead 4 to 5 times.

Roll dough to ¼-inch thickness; cut 18 biscuits using a 2-inch biscuit cutter and an additional 18 biscuits using a 1¼-inch biscuit cutter. Place larger biscuits 2 inches apart on an ungreased baking sheet; top each with a smaller biscuit. Cover and let rise in a warm place (85°), free from drafts, 1 hour or until doubled in bulk. Bake at 450° for 8 minutes. Brush tops with melted butter before serving. Yield: 1½ dozen.

VELVET BISCUITS

1 package dry yeast
⅓ cup warm water (105°
  to 115°)
1 cup warm milk (105°
  to 115°)
5 to 6 cups all-purpose
  flour, divided
3 eggs, beaten
2 tablespoons butter or
  margarine, melted
¼ cup sugar
1¼ teaspoons salt

Dissolve yeast in warm water; let stand 5 minutes or until bubbly. Combine warm milk and yeast mixture in a large bowl. Add 2 cups flour; stir until smooth. Cover and let rise in a warm place (85°), free from drafts, 1 hour or until doubled in bulk.

Add eggs, butter, sugar, salt, and enough remaining flour to make a soft dough, stirring until well blended.

Place dough in a greased bowl, turning to grease top. Cover and repeat rising procedure 1 hour.

Turn dough out onto a floured surface, and knead 3 to 4 minutes or until smooth. Roll dough to ½-inch thickness; cut with a 2-inch biscuit cutter. Place biscuits on greased baking sheets. Cover and repeat rising procedure for 1 hour or until doubled in bulk. Bake at 425° for 10 minutes or until biscuits are lightly browned. Yield: about 4 dozen.

Magic Yeast in a nineteenth-century advertisement.

FOR EVERY DAY AND SUNDAY

Antique cabinet shows off Topknot Biscuits (left) and Baking Powder Biscuits (right).

BAKING POWDER BISCUITS

2 cups all-purpose flour
1 tablespoon plus 1 teaspoon
  baking powder
¾ teaspoon salt
¼ cup plus 2 tablespoons
  shortening
¾ cup milk

Combine flour, baking powder, and salt; stir well. Cut in shortening until mixture resembles coarse meal. Sprinkle milk evenly over flour mixture, stirring until dry ingredients are moistened.

Turn dough out onto a floured surface; knead 10 to 12 times.

Roll dough to ¼-inch thickness; cut with a 1½-inch biscuit cutter. Place biscuits on greased baking sheets. Bake at 450° for 10 minutes or until lightly browned. Yield: 3½ dozen.

BISCUITS WITH SESAME SEEDS

2 cups all-purpose flour
1 tablespoon plus 1 teaspoon
  baking powder
1 teaspoon salt
3 tablespoons shortening
1 cup milk
Additional milk
2 tablespoons sesame seeds

Sift together flour, baking powder, and salt. Cut in shortening with a pastry blender until mixture resembles coarse meal. Sprinkle 1 cup milk evenly over flour mixture, stirring until dry ingredients are moistened.

Turn dough out onto a well-floured surface; knead lightly 10 to 12 times.

Roll dough to ½-inch thickness; cut with a 2-inch biscuit cutter. Place biscuits on a greased baking sheet. Brush each with milk, and sprinkle with sesame seeds. Bake at 450° for 12 minutes or until lightly browned. Yield: about 1 dozen.

Marjorie Kinnan Rawlings told a tale in *Cross Creek* of a Northerner who visited the South and never got to taste a hot Southern biscuit. He was a great talker, and as the biscuits were passed around, he would take one, butter it, put it down, and launch into conversation. As he reached for his biscuit, his hostess would say, "Oh no! You must have a hot one." She would ring for the biscuits to be brought in, the guest would take one, butter it, put it down, give forth only to have his biscuit snatched from him just as he was ready for it. As the tale goes, he left the South without experiencing one of its greatest delights.

Buttermilk Drop Biscuits (left) and Breakfast Biscuits (right).

BREAKFAST BISCUITS

2 cups all-purpose flour
1 tablespoon plus 1 teaspoon
   baking powder
½ teaspoon salt
3 tablespoons shortening
1 cup milk

Sift together flour, baking powder, and salt. Cut in shortening with a pastry blender until mixture resembles coarse meal. Sprinkle milk evenly over flour mixture, stirring until dry ingredients are moistened.

Turn dough out onto a well-floured surface; knead lightly 10 to 12 times.

Roll dough to ½-inch thickness; cut with a 2½-inch biscuit cutter. Place biscuits on a greased baking sheet. Bake at 450° for 12 minutes or until biscuits are lightly browned. Yield: 8 biscuits.

SODA BISCUITS

½ teaspoon baking soda
¾ cup buttermilk
2 cups sifted all-purpose flour
½ teaspoon salt
¼ cup plus 1 tablespoon
   shortening

Dissolve soda in buttermilk; stir well. Combine flour and salt; cut in shortening until mixture resembles coarse meal. Sprinkle buttermilk mixture evenly over flour mixture, stirring until dry ingredients are moistened.

Turn dough out onto a lightly floured surface; knead 4 to 5 times.

Roll dough to ½-inch thickness; cut with a 2-inch biscuit cutter. Place biscuits on a greased baking sheet. Bake at 475° for 10 minutes or until lightly browned. Yield: 1 dozen.

BUTTERMILK DROP BISCUITS

2 cups all-purpose flour
2 teaspoons baking
   powder
¼ teaspoon baking soda
1 teaspoon salt
¼ cup shortening
1 cup plus 2 tablespoons
   buttermilk

Sift together flour, baking powder, soda, and salt in a medium mixing bowl. Cut shortening into flour mixture with a pastry blender until mixture resembles coarse meal. Add buttermilk; stirring until dry ingredients are moistened.

Drop dough by tablespoonfuls 1½ inches apart onto greased baking sheets. Bake at 450° for 10 minutes or until biscuits are lightly browned. Yield: about 2 dozen.

SELF-RISING BUTTERMILK BISCUITS

2 cups self-rising flour
1½ teaspoons baking powder
1½ teaspoons sugar
¼ cup plus 2 tablespoons
  shortening
¾ to 1 cup buttermilk
2 tablespoons butter or
  margarine, melted

Combine flour, baking powder, and sugar; stir well. Cut in shortening until mixture resembles coarse meal. Gradually add buttermilk, stirring until dry ingredients are moistened.

Turn dough out onto a lightly floured surface, and knead 10 to 12 times.

Roll dough to ½-inch thickness; cut with a 3¼-inch biscuit cutter. Place biscuits on a greased baking sheet; brush with butter. Bake at 450° for 12 minutes or until lightly browned. Yield: 6 biscuits.

CATHEAD BISCUITS

2 cups all-purpose flour
1 tablespoon baking powder
¼ teaspoon baking soda
½ teaspoon salt
¼ cup plus 2 tablespoons
  butter or margarine
1 cup buttermilk
2 tablespoons butter or
  margarine, melted

Combine flour, baking powder, soda, and salt; stir well. Cut in ¼ cup plus 2 tablespoons butter until mixture resembles coarse meal. Sprinkle buttermilk evenly over flour mixture, stirring until dry ingredients are moistened.

Turn dough out onto a floured surface; knead 10 to 12 times.

Shape dough into 2-inch balls, and press with knuckles. Place biscuits on a greased baking sheet. Bake at 450° for 10 minutes. Brush tops of biscuits with melted butter, and continue baking an additional 2 minutes or until lightly browned. Yield: about 1 dozen.

VIRGINIA BUTTERMILK BISCUITS

2 cups all-purpose flour
2 teaspoons baking
  powder
1 teaspoon sugar
½ teaspoon salt
¼ cup plus 1 tablespoon
  shortening
½ teaspoon baking soda
1 cup buttermilk

Sift together flour, baking powder, sugar, and salt in a medium bowl. Cut in shortening with a pastry blender until mixture resembles coarse meal. Dissolve soda in buttermilk; pour evenly over flour mixture, stirring until dry ingredients are moistened.

Turn dough out onto a floured surface; knead 10 to 12 times.

Roll dough to ½-inch thickness; cut with a 2-inch biscuit cutter. Place biscuits on a greased baking sheet. Bake at 450° for 10 minutes or until lightly browned. Yield: about 1½ dozen.

Advertisement for Good Luck Baking Powder.

BASIC BISCUIT HOW-TO

Step 1—Accurately measure all dry
ingredients according to recipe.
Combine dry ingredients in a mixing bowl.
Stir with a fork to blend well.

Step 2—Cut in shortening
using a pastry blender
until mixture resembles
coarse meal.

Step 4—Turn dough out onto a
lightly floured surface. Using a
lightly floured rolling pin,
roll dough to desired thickness.

Step 5—Cut dough with a
biscuit cutter. Transfer
biscuits to a lightly greased
baking sheet and bake.

Step 3—Make a well in the center of mixture. Pour liquid into well. Stir until dry ingredients are moistened and dough is free from the sides of the bowl.

When biscuits are lightly browned, remove from oven. Immediately remove from baking sheet and serve hot with butter, if desired.

Sorghum-cutting photographed by Margaret W. Morley.

CHICKEN BISCUITS

1 cup all-purpose flour
2 teaspoons baking powder
¼ teaspoon salt
2 tablespoons butter or
  margarine, softened
½ cup milk
Vegetable oil
Cream gravy (optional)

Sift together dry ingredients; cut in butter until mixture resembles coarse meal. Add milk, stirring until dry ingredients are moistened.

Turn dough out onto a well-floured surface, and lightly knead 4 to 5 times.

Roll dough into a 7- x 5-inch rectangle; cut into thirty-five 1-inch squares. Heat 3 to 4 inches of oil to 375°; drop in 6 or 7 squares at a time. Cook 3 minutes on one side or until golden brown; turn and cook other side about 3 minutes. Drain. Serve with cream gravy, if desired. Yield: about 3 dozen.

Note: These are also delicious served with syrup or molasses.

COWBOY BISCUITS

The cowboy always made his biscuits with water, claiming that they were lighter and did not dry out as fast as milk-made ones.

2 cups all-purpose flour
2 teaspoons baking powder
½ teaspoon salt
¼ cup plus 1 tablespoon
  shortening
1 cup water
2 tablespoons bacon
  drippings, melted

Combine flour, baking powder, and salt; stir well. Cut in shortening until mixture resembles coarse meal. Sprinkle water over flour mixture; stir until dry ingredients are moistened.

Shape dough into 2-inch balls, and place on lightly greased baking sheets. Brush tops of biscuits with bacon drippings. Bake at 425° for 18 minutes or until lightly browned. Yield: 18 to 20 biscuits.

One of the Southerner's prime uses for hot biscuits (right after gravy) is to sop up cane syrup, sorghum, or molasses. Cane syrup and sorghum are made from ribbon cane; molasses is a by-product of sugar manufacture, much darker and stronger. Take your choice, but don't miss out on the joys of sopping. There are several ways to take part in this nourishing sport: Open several hot biscuits face up on your plate, butter them copiously, and pour on enough syrup to drench them well. Or pour a likely amount of syrup directly on the plate and mash into it a large chunk of firm butter; use as spread for biscuits. No fork? Poke a hole in the side of the biscuit with a finger, add a lump of butter and pour in syrup. Biscuits cold? Poke a hole in the side and pour in syrup. This last procedure delighted children as an after-school snack for generations.

BRAN BISCUITS

¾ cup buttermilk
½ cup shreds of wheat bran cereal
1½ cups all-purpose flour
1 teaspoon baking powder
½ teaspoon baking soda
½ teaspoon salt
⅓ cup shortening

Combine buttermilk and cereal; set aside. Sift together flour, baking powder, soda, and salt. Cut shortening into flour mixture with a pastry blender until mixture resembles coarse meal. Add cereal mixture, stirring with a fork until dry ingredients are moistened.

Turn dough out onto a floured surface; knead 4 to 5 times.

Roll dough to ½-inch thickness; cut with a 2½-inch biscuit cutter. Place biscuits on a greased baking sheet. Bake at 400° for 12 minutes or until biscuits are lightly browned. Yield: 8 biscuits.

SWEET POTATO BISCUITS

1 cup sifted all-purpose flour
1 tablespoon baking powder
½ teaspoon salt
3 tablespoons shortening
½ cup cooked, mashed sweet potatoes
¼ cup plus 2 tablespoons milk

Combine flour, baking powder, and salt; stir well. Cut in shortening until mixture resembles coarse meal. Stir in cooled potatoes. Sprinkle milk over flour mixture; stir until dry ingredients are moistened.

Turn dough out onto a lightly floured surface, and knead 10 to 12 times.

Roll dough to ½-inch thickness; cut with a 1¾-inch biscuit cutter. Place biscuits on a greased baking sheet. Bake at 450° for 8 minutes or until lightly browned. Yield: 1 dozen.

PEANUT BISCUITS

2⅓ cups all-purpose flour
¾ cup finely ground dry roasted peanuts
1 tablespoon plus 1 teaspoon baking powder
2 tablespoons sugar
1 teaspoon salt
¼ cup plus 1 tablespoon shortening
1 cup plus 2 tablespoons milk
Peanut butter (optional)
Grape jelly (optional)

Sift together flour, ground peanuts, baking powder, sugar, and salt. Cut in shortening until mixture resembles coarse meal. Add milk, stirring with a fork until dry ingredients are moistened.

Turn dough out onto a floured surface; knead 4 to 5 times.

Roll dough to ¾-inch thickness; cut with a 2-inch biscuit cutter. Place biscuits on greased baking sheets. Bake at 450° for 12 minutes or until lightly browned. Serve hot with peanut butter and jelly, if desired. Yield: about 2 dozen.

What do we serve with Peanut Biscuits? Jelly, naturally.

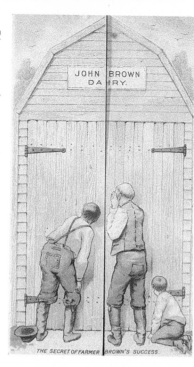

THE SECRET OF FARMER BROWN'S SUCCESS.

Attention-getting fold-out cards added suspense to advertising in the early 1900s. Of course, we want to know Farmer Brown's secret! Ah! His child does the work! Before the cream separator, cream was skimmed from the milk by hand, not an economical method. The separator, with centrifugal force, brought cream up and out in a hurry. It really was a time and labor saver for the small farmer as well as for the largest dairies.

WHIPPING CREAM BISCUITS

2 cups sifted all-purpose flour
1 tablespoon baking powder
1 teaspoon salt
1 cup whipping cream

Combine flour, baking powder, and salt; stir well. Beat whipping cream until soft peaks form; stir into flour mixture until well blended.

Turn dough out onto a lightly floured surface, and knead 10 to 12 times.

Roll dough to ½-inch thickness; cut with a 2-inch biscuit cutter. Place biscuits on a greased baking sheet. Bake at 450° for 12 minutes or until lightly browned. Yield: 1 dozen.

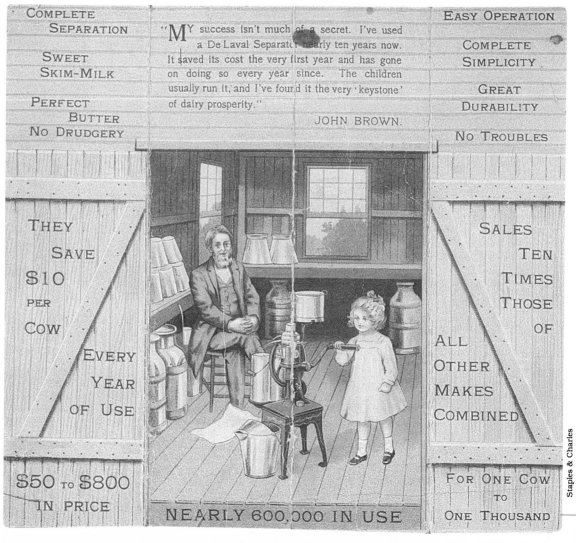

COMPLETE SEPARATION

SWEET SKIM-MILK

PERFECT BUTTER
NO DRUDGERY

"MY success isn't much of a secret. I've used a De Laval Separator nearly ten years now. It saved its cost the very first year and has gone on doing so every year since. The children usually run it, and I've found it the very 'keystone' of dairy prosperity."

JOHN BROWN.

EASY OPERATION

COMPLETE SIMPLICITY

GREAT DURABILITY

NO TROUBLES

THEY SAVE $10 PER COW EVERY YEAR OF USE

$50 TO $800 IN PRICE

NEARLY 600,000 IN USE

SALES TEN TIMES THOSE OF ALL OTHER MAKES COMBINED

FOR ONE COW TO ONE THOUSAND

Staples & Charles

RAISIN BISCUITS

3 cups all-purpose flour
1 tablespoon plus 1 teaspoon
   baking powder
1 tablespoon sugar
½ teaspoon salt
⅓ cup butter or margarine,
   softened
2 eggs, beaten
¾ cup milk
1½ cups raisins

Sift together dry ingredients; cut in butter with a pastry blender until mixture resembles coarse meal. Add eggs and milk, stirring until well blended. Stir in raisins.

Turn dough out onto a well-floured surface, and lightly knead 7 to 8 times.

Roll dough to ½-inch thickness; cut with a 2-inch biscuit cutter. Place biscuits on greased baking sheets. Bake at 400° for 12 minutes or until lightly browned. Yield: about 2 dozen.

SWEET BISCUITS

2 cups all-purpose flour
1 tablespoon plus 1 teaspoon
   baking powder
2 teaspoons sugar
½ teaspoon salt
⅓ cup butter or margarine
⅔ cup plus 2 tablespoons
   milk

Combine flour, baking powder, sugar, and salt in a large bowl. Cut in butter with a pastry blender until mixture resembles coarse meal. Add milk, stirring until dry ingredients are moistened.

Turn dough out onto a lightly floured surface. Flour hands, and shape dough into 1½-inch balls. Place biscuits 1½ inches apart on a greased baking sheet. Bake at 400° for 20 minutes or until lightly browned. Yield: about 1½ dozen.

Skon Bread: A fry-pan bread good as a shortcake base or plain, hot off the campfire.

SKON BREAD

1 cup all-purpose flour
1 teaspoon baking powder
¼ teaspoon salt
1 tablespoon shortening
¼ cup milk
**Strawberries and whipped
   cream (optional)**

Combine flour, baking powder, and salt; stir well. Cut in shortening until mixture resembles coarse meal. Sprinkle milk evenly over flour mixture, stir-

ring until dry ingredients are moistened.

Turn dough out onto a floured surface; knead 10 to 12 times.

Roll dough to ¼-inch thickness; cut into four 4½-inch circles. Place on a hot greased griddle or skillet; cook over medium heat 2 minutes on each side or until lightly browned. Serve warm with strawberries and whipped cream, if desired. Yield: 2 servings.

Time for tea, White Sulphur Springs, West Virginia, early 1900s.

ANGEL FOOD BISCUITS

2½ cups all-purpose flour,
  divided
1 tablespoon baking powder
½ teaspoon salt
¼ cup butter or margarine,
  softened
¾ cup milk
2 egg whites

Combine 2 cups flour, baking powder, and salt; stir well. Cut in butter until mixture resembles coarse meal. Sprinkle milk evenly over flour mixture, stirring just until dry ingredients are moistened.

Beat egg whites (at room temperature) until stiff peaks form; fold into flour mixture. Sprinkle remaining flour evenly over kneading surface. Turn dough out onto a floured surface; knead lightly 10 to 12 times.

Roll dough to ½-inch thickness; cut with a 2-inch biscuit cutter. Place biscuits on a greased baking sheet. Bake at 450° for 12 minutes or until lightly browned. Yield: 1½ dozen.

BENNE SEED BISCUITS

2 cups sifted all-purpose flour
1 teaspoon baking powder
½ teaspoon salt
½ cup sesame seeds, toasted
½ cup shortening
¾ cup milk

Combine flour, baking powder, salt, and sesame seeds; stir well. Cut in shortening until mixture resembles coarse meal. Sprinkle milk evenly over flour mixture, stirring until dry ingredients are moistened.

Turn dough out onto a lightly floured surface; knead 4 to 5 times.

Roll dough to ¼-inch thickness; cut with a 1¾-inch biscuit cutter. Place biscuits on greased baking sheets. Bake at 350° for 12 minutes or until lightly browned. Yield: about 3 dozen.

CARAWAY BRAN BISCUITS

1½ cups all-purpose flour
1 teaspoon baking powder
½ teaspoon baking soda
1 teaspoon salt
½ cup shreds of wheat bran cereal
½ cup (2 ounces) shredded sharp Cheddar cheese
1½ teaspoons caraway seeds
⅓ cup shortening
¾ cup buttermilk

Combine flour, baking powder, soda, and salt; stir well. Add cereal, cheese, and caraway seeds, stirring well. Cut in shortening. Sprinkle buttermilk evenly over flour mixture, stirring until dry ingredients are moistened.

Turn dough out onto a lightly floured surface; knead 4 to 6 times.

Roll dough to ½-inch thickness; cut with a 1¾-inch biscuit cutter. Place biscuits on ungreased baking sheets. Bake at 450° for 10 minutes or until lightly browned. Yield: about 2 dozen.

Tea drinking in this country just never was the same after the Boston Tea Party. Americans now drink about twenty-five cups of coffee for every cup of tea consumed. East Asian tea gardens go back to about 2700 B.C., but the English had to wait for the East India Company to bring it home in the seventeenth century.

The British spread tea culture to India and Ceylon; the Dutch took it to Java. This country is right behind England in the importation of tea. Black tea or green, iced or hot, there is real refreshment in tea, and Southerners like to dream up things like party biscuits flavored with caraway or benne seeds or cheese or cinnamon to go with it.

Benne Seed Biscuits (rear) and Caraway Bran Biscuits (front).

CINNAMON BISCUIT ROLLS

4 cups all-purpose flour
2 tablespoons plus 2 teaspoons baking powder
1 teaspoon salt
¼ cup plus 2 tablespoons shortening
1½ cups milk
3 tablespoons butter or margarine, melted
¼ cup plus 2 tablespoons sugar
¾ teaspoon ground cinnamon
1 cup sifted powdered sugar
2 tablespoons milk

Combine flour, baking powder, and salt; stir well. Cut in shortening until mixture resembles coarse meal. Sprinkle 1½ cups milk evenly over flour mixture, stirring until dry ingredients are moistened.

Turn dough out onto a lightly floured surface; knead 10 to 12 times.

Roll dough out to a ¼-inch thick 15- x 11-inch rectangle; brush with melted butter.

Combine sugar and cinnamon; sprinkle over dough. Roll up jellyroll fashion, beginning at long side; moisten edges with water to seal. Cut roll into twenty-two ½-inch slices; place slices, cut side down, on greased baking sheets. Bake at 400° for 15 minutes or until rolls are lightly browned.

Combine powdered sugar and 2 tablespoons milk, beating well. Drizzle over warm rolls. Yield: about 2 dozen.

Cinnamon branch and fruit.

CHEESE BISCUIT THINS

1 cup all-purpose flour
2 teaspoons baking powder
¼ teaspoon salt
2 tablespoons shortening
½ cup milk
⅔ cup (2½ ounces) shredded sharp Cheddar cheese
Paprika
Melted butter or shortening

Combine flour, baking powder, and salt; stir well. Cut in shortening until mixture resembles coarse meal. Sprinkle milk evenly over flour mixture, stirring until dry ingredients are moistened.

Turn dough out onto a lightly floured surface; knead 4 to 5 times.

Roll dough to a 12- x 10-inch rectangle. Sprinkle cheese and paprika over half the dough, leaving about a ¼-inch margin at edges. Fold dough over cheese; pinch edges to seal.

Roll dough to a 10- x 8-inch rectangle; cut into 4- x 1-inch strips, and place on a greased baking sheet. Brush each strip with melted butter. Bake at 400° for 10 minutes or until lightly browned. Yield: about 1½ dozen.

CHEESE ROUNDS

3 cups all-purpose flour
½ teaspoon salt
⅛ teaspoon red pepper
½ teaspoon paprika
1 cup butter or margarine, softened
2 cups (8 ounces) shredded sharp Cheddar cheese

Combine flour, salt, pepper, and paprika; stir well. Cut in butter until mixture resembles coarse meal. Add cheese; stir well. Shape into a ball.

Roll dough to ⅓-inch thickness on a floured surface; cut with a 1¾-inch biscuit cutter. Place biscuits on greased baking sheets. Bake at 450° for 15 minutes. Yield: about 4 dozen.

COCKTAIL BISCUITS

2½ cups all-purpose flour
1 tablespoon plus 1 teaspoon baking powder
1 tablespoon sugar
1 teaspoon salt
⅓ cup shortening
¾ cup milk
1 egg
3 tablespoons butter or margarine, softened

Combine flour, baking powder, sugar, and salt; stir well. Cut in shortening until mixture resembles coarse meal. Combine milk and egg, beating well. Pour milk mixture evenly over flour mixture, stirring until dry ingredients are moistened.

Turn dough out onto a floured surface; knead 10 to 12 times.

Roll dough to ¼-inch thickness; cut with a 1½-inch biscuit cutter. Spread biscuits with softened butter; make a crease with a knife across each circle and fold in half. Press edges to seal. Place on greased baking sheets. Bake at 450° for 10 minutes or until biscuits are lightly browned. Yield: 5½ dozen.

For teatime or snacktime, think biscuit variations: Try Cocktail Biscuits (left), Cinnamon Biscuit Rolls (top), or Cheese Rounds (center).

Drop Biscuit.

Beat the yolks of 10 eggs, and the whites of six: 3/4 lb. of white sugar: 6 ounces of flour. Stir in the flour gently. Drop them softly on paper and bake in a moderate oven.

Drop Biscuits from illustrated manuscript, Recipes in the Culinary Art, *1852.*

FRUIT DROP BISCUITS

2 cups all-purpose flour
2½ teaspoons baking powder
2 tablespoons sugar
½ teaspoon salt
¼ cup butter or margarine, softened
1 cup finely chopped apples
½ cup raisins, finely chopped
1½ teaspoons grated orange rind
¾ cup milk

Combine flour, baking powder, sugar, and salt; stir well. Cut in butter until mixture resembles coarse meal. Add apples, raisins, and rind; stir well. Sprinkle milk evenly over flour mixture, stirring until dry ingredients are moistened.

Drop batter by teaspoonfuls onto greased baking sheets. Bake at 450° for 8 minutes or until lightly browned. Yield: about 3½ dozen.

CRESCENT TEA BISCUITS

2 cups all-purpose flour
2 teaspoons baking powder
2 teaspoons sugar
½ teaspoon salt
2 tablespoons lard
1 tablespoon butter
1 egg yolk, beaten
½ cup plus 2 tablespoons milk
2 tablespoons butter or margarine, melted

Combine flour, baking powder, sugar, and salt; stir well. Cut in lard and butter until mixture resembles coarse meal. Add egg yolk and milk to flour mixture, stirring until dry ingredients are moistened. Turn dough out onto a lightly floured surface; knead 10 to 12 times.

Roll dough to ¼-inch thickness. Cut into 2-inch circles, and brush with 1 tablespoon melted butter. Make a crease across each circle, and fold one half over. Gently press edges to seal; brush tops with remaining butter. Place on greased baking sheets. Bake at 450° for 12 minutes or until lightly browned. Yield: about 2 dozen.

SWEET ORANGE ROLL-UPS

¼ cup plus 2 tablespoons
  butter or margarine
3 tablespoons all-purpose
  flour
2 tablespoons grated
  orange rind
⅓ cup orange juice
½ cup sugar
2 cups all-purpose flour
1 tablespoon plus 1 teaspoon
  baking powder
½ teaspoon salt
3 tablespoons shortening
1 cup milk

Melt butter in a heavy sauce-pan over low heat; add 3 table-spoons flour, stirring until smooth. Stir in orange rind and juice; cook over medium heat, stirring constantly, until thick-ened and bubbly. Remove from heat; add sugar, stirring until sugar is dissolved. Set mixture aside to cool.

Sift together 2 cups flour, baking powder, and salt; cut in shortening with a pastry blender until mixture resembles coarse meal. Add milk, stirring just until dry ingredients are moistened.

Turn dough out onto a well-floured surface, kneading lightly until dough is smooth. Roll dough to a ¼-inch thick 15- x 10-inch rectangle. Spread ¾ cup of orange-sugar mixture evenly over dough, reserving ½ cup; leave a narrow margin on all sides. Roll up jellyroll fash-ion, beginning at long side. Cut roll into eighteen ¾-inch slices; gently place slices, cut side down, in well-greased muffin pans. Bake at 400° for 18 min-utes or until rolls are lightly browned. Remove from pan and drizzle warm rolls with reserved orange-sugar mixture. Yield: about 1½ dozen.

For a backyard tea party, serve Florida Orange Biscuits (rear) and Sweet Orange Roll-Ups (front).

FLORIDA ORANGE BISCUITS

2 cups all-purpose flour
2 teaspoons baking powder
1 tablespoon sugar
½ teaspoon salt
1 teaspoon grated orange rind
2 tablespoons butter or
  margarine, softened
¾ cup orange juice
½ cup milk
½ teaspoon sugar
1 tablespoon orange juice

Combine flour, baking pow-der, 1 tablespoon sugar, and salt; stir well. Add rind, and stir well. Cut in butter until mixture resembles coarse meal. Add ¾ cup orange juice and milk, stir-ring until dry ingredients are moistened. Turn dough out onto a lightly floured surface; knead 10 to 12 times.

Roll dough to ½-inch thick-ness; cut with a 1¾-inch biscuit cutter. Place biscuits on lightly greased baking sheets.

Combine remaining ingre-dients; stir well. Gently press thumb into center of each bis-cuit. Spoon sugar-orange juice mixture into depressions. Bake at 450° for 10 minutes or until lightly browned. Yield: 2½ dozen.

QUICK DELIGHTS

H ere's a chapterful of breads so quick that the busy cook can accomplish almost any one of them in about an hour. One notable exception: Brown Bread that has to steam for three hours. But think of it as three hours gained for another activity! Make the Banana Nut Bread we inherited from Corrie Hill, a descendant of George Washington's uncle. Or try a loaf of Applesauce Nut Bread that has stood the tests of time and thousands of customers at Casselman Inn on Main Street in Grantsville, Maryland. The Inn has been there since 1824, when it was a stopover for settlers traveling west on the National Trail. Guests still awaken to the aroma of baking bread which drifts through the inn during the early morning hours.

Non-yeast loaves such as these are popular in the South, where they are often served in thin slices sandwiched with cream cheese mixtures for party trays. Alternatively, they simply can be sliced warm and wolfed down by hungry children and other alert gourmands.

At one time, muffins were the tastiest stock-in-trade of the old-fashioned tearoom. Hostesses still realize that one lilting gem of a hot muffin can elevate an otherwise simple luncheon or supper to the heights. If muffins seem appropriate, dip into the recipe files of famous places, private and public, from Shirley Plantation on the James River to Memphis' fabled Peabody Hotel. Turn to Pumpkin Muffins à la Greenbrier, the stunning West Virginia resort hotel, or to the Orange Blossom Muffins that have kept guests enchanted for so long at the Excelsior House in Jefferson, Texas.

In 1961, a group of volunteers known as the Jesse Allen Wise Garden Club rescued the then-decrepit 1854-vintage Excelsior House and restored it to the state of grace it enjoyed in the days when the likes of Jay Gould, John Jacob Astor, and Oscar Wilde reveled in its hospitality. Presidents' names appear, too, in the hotel register: Ulysses S. Grant, Rutherford B. Hayes, and Lyndon B. Johnson.

Then there are the sweet bakings that make a party out of a hot cup of coffee, whether on a leisurely Sunday morning at home or at a working business meeting. Streusel-topped or drizzled with icing, cut in squares, slices, wedges, they are all balms to the Southerner's famous sweet tooth.

Glazed Cinnamon Ring sits in front of antique Shaker-made basket filled with Squash Muffins. Lemon Bread loaves, sliced and unsliced, complete picture taken in original bake-kitchen at Shakertown at Pleasant Hill, Kentucky.

BAKING POWDER BREAD

4 cups all-purpose flour
2 tablespoons baking powder
1 tablespoon sugar
1½ teaspoons salt
2 cups milk
¼ cup lard, melted

Sift together dry ingredients. Combine milk and lard; add to dry ingredients, stirring just until moistened.

Spoon batter into 2 greased 7½- x 3- x 2-inch loafpans. Bake at 400° for 30 minutes or until lightly browned. Remove bread from pans immediately; cool on wire racks. Yield: 2 loaves.

GOLDEN BROWN BREAD

2 cups sifted whole wheat flour
1 cup cornmeal
2 teaspoons baking powder
¼ teaspoon baking soda
1 teaspoon salt
1¼ cups sorghum molasses
1 cup milk
1 cup raisins

Combine dry ingredients in a large mixing bowl; make a well in center of mixture. Combine molasses and milk; add to dry ingredients, stirring just until moistened. Stir in raisins.

Pour batter into a well-greased 1½-quart pudding mold, and cover tightly with a lid. Place mold on rack in a large kettle; add boiling water, filling kettle half full. Bring to a boil; cover and simmer 3 hours.

Remove mold from kettle; remove lid from mold to allow steam to escape. Cool slightly. Loosen bread from sides of mold, and invert onto serving dish. Cool completely. Yield: 8 to 10 servings.

Golden Brown Bread (front) and Quick Sally Lunn.

QUICK SALLY LUNN

2 tablespoons butter or margarine, softened
2 tablespoons sugar
2 eggs, separated
2 cups sifted all-purpose flour
1 teaspoon cream of tartar
½ teaspoon baking soda
¼ teaspoon salt
½ cup milk

Cream butter; gradually add sugar, beating until light and fluffy. Add egg yolks; beat well.

Combine flour, cream of tartar, soda, and salt; add to creamed mixture alternately with milk, beginning and ending with flour mixture. Mix well after each addition.

Beat egg whites (at room temperature) until stiff peaks form; fold into batter. Spoon into a greased 6-cup Bundt pan. Bake at 400° for 25 minutes or until golden brown. Cool 10 minutes. Remove from pan; cool on wire rack. Yield: one 8-inch loaf.

Nineteenth-century booklet cover.

WHOLE WHEAT QUICK BREAD

2 cups whole wheat flour
½ cup firmly packed brown
  sugar
1 teaspoon baking powder
1 teaspoon baking soda
¾ teaspoon salt
1 egg, beaten
1½ cups buttermilk
½ cup raisins
½ cup chopped pecans

Combine first 5 ingredients; stir well. Add egg and buttermilk; mix well. Stir in raisins and pecans. Spoon into a greased and floured 8- x 4- x 3-inch loafpan. Bake at 350° for 55 minutes or until a wooden pick inserted in center comes out clean. Cool 10 minutes; remove from pan and cool completely. Yield: 1 loaf.

WHOLE WHEAT SQUARES

1 egg, beaten
1 cup milk
2 tablespoons honey
¾ cup whole wheat flour
⅔ cup cornmeal
2½ teaspoons baking powder
3 tablespoons shortening,
  melted
Butter or margarine
Honey

Combine egg, milk, and 2 tablespoons honey; beat well. Combine flour, cornmeal, and baking powder; add to egg mixture, mixing well. Add melted shortening; mix batter well.

Pour into a greased 8-inch square baking pan. Bake at 425° for 20 minutes or until wooden pick inserted in center comes out clean. Cut into 2-inch squares; serve with butter and honey. Yield: 16 servings.

WHOLE WHEAT HONEY BREAD

1 cup milk
½ cup honey
1 egg, beaten
2 tablespoons butter, melted
1 cup whole wheat flour
1 cup sifted all-purpose
  flour
2½ teaspoons baking
  powder
½ teaspoon salt

Combine milk, honey, egg, and butter; beat well.

Sift together dry ingredients in a large bowl; add milk mixture, stirring well.

Spoon batter into a greased 7½- x 3- x 2-inch loafpan. Bake at 350° for 1 hour and 15 minutes or until a wooden pick inserted in center comes out clean. Cool in pan 10 minutes; remove from pan, and cool on wire rack. Yield: 1 loaf.

PHILPY

An old-time recipe that, because of the rice, has neither the appearance nor texture of traditional quick breads.

½ cup all-purpose flour
½ teaspoon salt
½ cup milk
¾ cup cooked rice, mashed
2 teaspoons butter or margarine, melted
1 egg, beaten

Combine flour and salt in a mixing bowl. Gradually add milk, stirring until mixture is smooth. Add rice, butter, and egg; mix well. Spoon mixture into a lightly greased 8-inch round cakepan. Bake at 450° for 25 minutes or until lightly browned. Yield: 4 to 6 servings.

CASSELMAN INN APPLESAUCE NUT BREAD

¾ cup sugar
1¼ cups applesauce
3 tablespoons vegetable oil
2 eggs, beaten
2 cups all-purpose flour
1 tablespoon baking powder
½ teaspoon baking soda
1 teaspoon salt
¾ teaspoon ground cinnamon
¼ teaspoon ground cloves
¾ cup chopped pecans

Combine sugar, applesauce, oil, and eggs in a large mixing bowl; beat at medium speed of electric mixer 1 minute. Set mixture aside.

Combine flour, baking powder, soda, salt, and spices; add to applesauce mixture, beating until smooth. Stir in pecans.

Spoon batter into a greased 8½- x 4½- x 3-inch loafpan. Bake at 375° for 50 minutes or until a wooden pick inserted in center comes out clean. Cool in pan 10 minutes; remove from pan, and cool on a wire rack. Yield: 1 loaf.

1873 poster
idealizes the farmer.

CORRIE HILL'S BANANA NUT BREAD

Mrs. Hill's great-great-grandfather was George Washington's uncle.

½ cup butter or margarine, softened
1 cup sugar
2 eggs
1½ cups puréed bananas (4 medium bananas)
2 cups all-purpose flour
1 teaspoon baking soda
¼ teaspoon salt
1 cup chopped pecans

Cream butter; gradually add sugar, beating well. Add eggs, one at a time, beating well after each addition. Add puréed bananas, and mix until smooth.

Combine flour, soda, and salt; add to creamed mixture, stirring just until dry ingredients are moistened. Stir in pecans.

Pour batter into 2 greased 7½- x 3- x 2-inch loafpans. Bake at 375° for 15 minutes; reduce heat to 350°, and bake an additional 40 minutes or until a wooden pick inserted in center comes out clean. Cool in pans 10 minutes; remove from pans, and cool completely on wire racks. Yield: 2 loaves.

Banana Nut Bread (rear) and Applesauce Nut Bread.

Marmalade Nut Bread: Try it buttered and toasted.

LEMON BREAD

⅓ cup shortening
1 cup sugar
2 eggs
1½ cups sifted all-purpose
  flour
1½ teaspoons baking powder
¼ teaspoon salt
½ cup milk
Grated rind of 1 lemon
½ cup chopped pecans
  (optional)
⅓ cup sugar
Juice of 1 lemon

Cream shortening; gradually add 1 cup sugar, beating well. Add eggs, one at a time, beating well after each addition.

Combine flour, baking powder, and salt; add to creamed mixture alternately with milk, beginning and ending with flour mixture. Mix well after each addition. Stir in rind and pecans, if desired.

Pour batter into a greased 8½- x 4½- x 3-inch loafpan. Bake at 350° for 50 minutes or until a

wooden pick inserted in center comes out clean.

Combine ⅓ cup sugar and lemon juice, stirring well; immediately pour over bread in pan. Cool in pan 10 minutes; remove from pan, and cool completely on wire rack. Yield: 1 loaf.

MARMALADE NUT BREAD

3 cups all-purpose flour
½ cup sugar
1 tablespoon baking powder
½ teaspoon salt
2 eggs, beaten
1 cup milk
1 cup chopped pecans or
  walnuts
½ cup shortening, melted
½ cup orange marmalade
1 tablespoon grated orange
  rind
Cream cheese, softened
  (optional)

Sift together flour, sugar, baking powder, and salt; stir in remaining ingredients, except cream cheese, just until dry ingredients are moistened.

Spoon mixture into a greased 9- x 5- x 3-inch loafpan. Bake at 350° for 1 hour. Cool in pan 10 minutes; remove from pan, and cool completely on a wire rack. Spread slices with cream cheese, if desired. Yield: 1 loaf.

OLD-FASHIONED NUT LOAF

⅔ cup butter or margarine, softened
1 cup sugar
3 eggs
2 cups sifted cake flour
2 teaspoons baking powder
½ teaspoon salt
⅓ cup milk
1 cup finely chopped pecans
1 teaspoon vanilla extract

Cream butter; gradually add sugar, beating until light and fluffy. Add eggs, one at a time, beating well after each addition.

Sift together flour, baking powder, and salt; repeat sifting, and add to creamed mixture alternately with milk, beginning and ending with flour mixture. Mix just until blended. Gently stir in pecans and vanilla.

Spoon batter into a greased 8½- x 4½- x 3-inch loafpan. Bake at 350° for 1 hour or until wooden pick inserted in center comes out clean. Cool in pan 10 minutes; remove from pan, and cool completely on wire rack. Yield: 1 loaf.

PEANUT BUTTER BREAD

1 teaspoon baking soda
1 cup buttermilk
2 cups all-purpose flour
2 teaspoons baking powder
½ cup sugar
1 teaspoon salt
1 cup peanut butter
2 eggs, beaten

Dissolve soda in buttermilk, stirring well; set aside.

Sift together dry ingredients in a large bowl; make a well in center of mixture. Combine buttermilk mixture, peanut butter, and eggs; mix well. Add to dry ingredients, stirring just until moistened.

Spoon batter into a greased 8½- x 4½- x 3-inch loafpan. Bake at 350° for 55 minutes or until a wooden pick inserted in center comes out clean. Cool 10 minutes. Remove from pan, and cool completely. Yield: 1 loaf.

FLORIDA ORANGE BREAD

1 cup finely chopped orange rind (about 4 small oranges)
1 cup sugar
½ cup water
2½ cups all-purpose flour
1 tablespoon baking powder
⅔ cup sugar
½ teaspoon salt
1 egg, beaten
1 cup milk

Combine orange rind, sugar, and water in a heavy saucepan; bring to a boil. Reduce heat, and simmer 25 minutes, stirring frequently. Remove from heat; drain orange rind, and set aside to cool. Reserve liquid; set aside and let cool.

Sift together flour, baking powder, sugar, and salt in a large bowl. Combine reserved orange liquid, egg, and milk; add to flour mixture, stirring just until dry ingredients are moistened. Stir in orange rind.

Pour batter into a greased 9- x 5- x 3-inch loafpan. Bake at 350° for 1 hour or until wooden pick inserted in center comes out clean. Cool 10 minutes. Remove from pan; cool completely on wire rack. Yield: 1 loaf.

PERSIMMON NUT BREAD

1¾ cups all-purpose flour
1 teaspoon baking soda
¾ teaspoon salt
½ teaspoon ground mace
1¼ cups sugar
2 eggs, beaten
⅓ cup bourbon
1 cup persimmon pulp, puréed
½ cup butter or margarine, softened
1 cup raisins
1 cup chopped pecans

Combine flour, soda, salt, and mace; set aside.

Combine sugar, eggs, bourbon, and persimmon pulp; mix well. Add persimmon mixture and butter to flour mixture, mixing well. Stir in raisins and pecans.

Spoon batter into a greased and floured 6-cup mold. Bake at 350° for 1 hour and 35 minutes or until a wooden pick inserted in center comes out clean. Cool 15 to 20 minutes in mold. Remove from mold, and cool completely. Yield: 1 loaf.

Persimmons, or date plums, used in much of our baking.

Prune Bread: Here served with cream cheese.

PUMPKIN BREAD

3⅓ cups all-purpose flour
3 cups sugar
2 teaspoons baking soda
1½ teaspoons salt
1 tablespoon ground
  cinnamon
1 tablespoon ground nutmeg
½ teaspoon ground ginger
1 (18-ounce) can pumpkin pie
  mix
1 cup vegetable oil
⅔ cup water
4 eggs, slightly beaten

Combine dry ingredients; stir well. Add pie mix, oil, water, and eggs; beat 2 minutes at medium speed of electric mixer.

Spoon batter into 2 greased and floured 9- x 5- x 3-inch loafpans. Bake at 350° for 1 hour and 40 minutes or until a wooden pick inserted in center comes out clean. Cool 10 minutes; remove from pans and cool completely. Yield: 2 loaves.

SWEET POTATO BREAD

2 cups all-purpose flour
1¼ teaspoons baking soda
1 cup sugar
¾ teaspoon salt
1 teaspoon ground cinnamon
1 teaspoon ground cloves
⅓ cup vegetable oil
¼ cup milk
2 eggs
1 cup cooked, mashed sweet
  potatoes
⅔ cup raisins
⅔ cup chopped pecans

Sift together dry ingredients and spices; make a well in center of mixture. Set aside.

Combine oil, milk, and eggs; mix well. Stir in potatoes, raisins, and pecans; add to dry ingredients, stirring just until moistened.

Spoon mixture into a well-greased 8½- x 4½- x 3-inch loafpan. Bake at 350° for 1 hour and 15 minutes or until a wooden pick inserted in center comes out clean. Cool in pan 10 minutes; remove from pan, and cool completely. Yield: 1 loaf.

PRUNE BREAD

2 (8-ounce) packages pitted
  prunes, chopped
4 cups water
2 cups sugar
¾ cup lard
1 teaspoon ground cinnamon
1 teaspoon ground cloves
½ teaspoon salt
4 cups sifted all-purpose flour
2 teaspoons baking soda
2 eggs, beaten

Combine prunes and water in a large bowl; cover and refrigerate overnight. Drain prunes, reserving 2 cups liquid.

Combine prunes, reserved liquid, sugar, lard, spices, and salt in a large saucepan. Cook over medium heat, stirring occasionally, 10 minutes or until lard melts. Remove from heat, and let cool.

Sift together flour and soda in a medium mixing bowl; add prune mixture and eggs, stirring just until dry ingredients are moistened.

Pour batter into 2 greased 9- x 5- x 3-inch loafpans. Bake at 350° for 1 hour or until a wooden pick inserted in center comes out clean. Cool in pans 10 minutes; remove from pans, and cool completely on wire racks. Yield: 2 loaves.

MUFFINS IN MINUTES

MINIATURE LUNCHEON MUFFINS

⅓ cup butter or margarine,
  softened
⅓ cup sugar
1 egg
1½ cups all-purpose flour
1 tablespoon baking powder
¼ teaspoon salt
½ cup milk

Cream butter; gradually add sugar, beating until light and fluffy. Add egg, and beat mixture until well blended.

Combine flour, baking powder, and salt; add to creamed mixture alternately with milk, beginning and ending with flour mixture.

Spoon batter into greased miniature muffin pans, filling two-thirds full. Bake at 400° for 12 minutes or until lightly browned. Yield: 3 dozen.

DINNER MUFFINS

2 cups sifted all-purpose flour
2½ teaspoons baking powder
2 teaspoons sugar
1 teaspoon salt
½ cup butter or margarine,
  melted
2 eggs, beaten
¼ cup milk

Sift together dry ingredients in a medium mixing bowl. Add butter and eggs; mix well. Add milk, stirring just until dry ingredients are moistened.

Spoon batter into greased miniature muffin pans, filling two-thirds full. Bake at 400° for 12 minutes or until lightly browned. Yield: about 3 dozen.

SOUR CREAM MUFFINS

2 cups sifted all-purpose flour
1 tablespoon baking powder
1 teaspoon baking soda
1 tablespoon sugar
¾ teaspoon salt
1½ cups commercial sour
  cream
1 egg, beaten

Sift together dry ingredients in a medium mixing bowl. Gradually add sour cream and egg, stirring well.

Spoon batter into greased miniature muffin pans, filling two-thirds full. Bake at 400° for 12 minutes or until lightly browned. Yield: about 4 dozen.

Miniature Luncheon Muffins: That "something" extra.

PATENT.
EGG AND CREAM BEATER.

Opened in Memphis in 1869, The Peabody Hotel was rebuilt in 1925.

THE PEABODY'S VANILLA MUFFINS

2 cups sugar
4 eggs, beaten
4 cups all-purpose flour
1 tablespoon baking powder
2 cups milk
½ cup butter, melted
1 tablespoon vanilla extract

Combine sugar and eggs; beat until well blended.

Combine flour and baking powder. Add to sugar mixture alternately with milk, beginning and ending with flour mixture; beat after each addition. Add butter and vanilla.

Place greased muffin pans in a 400° oven for 3 minutes. Spoon batter into pans; fill two-thirds full. Bake at 400° about 20 minutes. Yield: 3 dozen.

The recently restored Peabody Hotel is known for its Duck Ceremony, which began in the 1930s as a prank. A couple of hunters returned to the hotel and tossed their call ducks into the fountain. (Live decoys were legal then.) Onlookers were so amused that the daily Duck Walk became a part of Peabody life, captivating guests ever since. From their home atop the hotel, the ducks descend by elevator at 11 a.m. and file across a red carpet to the fountain.

Easy, tempting Popovers.

POPOVERS

2 eggs
1 cup all-purpose flour
1 cup milk
1 tablespoon butter or
   margarine, melted
½ teaspoon salt

Beat eggs with electric mixer until light and fluffy. Add flour and milk alternately, beginning and ending with flour; beat well after each addition. Stir in butter and salt.

Heat a well-greased muffin pan in a 450° oven for 3 minutes or until very hot. Spoon batter into muffin pans, filling two-thirds full. Bake at 425° for 20 minutes; reduce heat to 350°, and bake an additional 20 minutes. Serve immediately. Yield: 8 popovers.

The climate in Asheville, North Carolina, is so salubrious that meteorologists dream of retiring there. Early this century, Edwin Wiley Grove left his Tennessee home to settle in Asheville for health reasons. When he opened the Grove Park Inn in 1913, the menus reflected some of his ideas on eating for health's sake. Bran muffins from the resort's earliest bills of fare are still served there. The 200-room inn was placed on the National Register of Historic Places in 1973.

SHIRLEY GRAHAM MUFFINS

1 cup whole wheat flour
½ cup all-purpose flour
1½ teaspoons baking
   powder
3 tablespoons sugar
¼ teaspoon salt
½ cup butter or margarine,
   melted
2 eggs, beaten
½ cup milk

Sift together flour, baking powder, sugar, and salt in a medium mixing bowl. Add butter, eggs, and milk; stir just until dry ingredients are moistened.

Spoon batter into well-greased muffin pans, filling three-fourths full. Bake at 400° for 20 minutes or until golden brown. Yield: 1 dozen.

GROVE PARK INN BRAN MUFFINS

1 cup bran
½ cup whole wheat flour
½ cup all-purpose flour
1½ teaspoons baking powder
½ teaspoon salt
2 eggs, beaten
2 tablespoons butter or
   margarine, melted
1 cup milk
¼ cup honey

Combine dry ingredients in a large mixing bowl, stirring well. Make a well in center of mixture. Combine eggs, butter, milk, and honey; add to dry ingredients, stirring just until dry ingredients are moistened.

Spoon batter into greased muffin pans, filling two-thirds full. Bake at 400° for 20 minutes. Yield: 1 dozen.

CHARLESTON RICE MUFFINS

½ cup butter or margarine,
   softened
1 cup sugar
2 eggs
2 cups flour
1 tablespoon baking powder
1 cup milk
1 cup cooked regular rice

Cream butter; gradually add sugar, beating well. Add eggs, one at a time, beating well after each addition.

Combine flour and baking powder; add to creamed mixture alternately with milk, beginning and ending with flour mixture. Fold rice into batter.

Spoon batter into greased muffin pans, filling two-thirds full. Bake at 425° for 20 minutes or until lightly browned. Yield: about 1½ dozen.

APPLESAUCE MUFFINS

1¾ cups applesauce
1 egg, beaten
1 cup plus 1 tablespoon
   all-purpose flour, divided
1 cup whole wheat flour
1 teaspoon baking soda
¼ cup sugar
½ teaspoon salt
½ cup raisins
3 tablespoons shortening,
   melted

Combine applesauce and egg in a mixing bowl; stir well. Combine 1 cup all-purpose flour, whole wheat flour, soda, sugar, and salt; add to applesauce mixture, stirring just until dry ingredients are moistened.

Dredge raisins in remaining 1 tablespoon all-purpose flour. Add raisins and shortening to batter, stirring just until blended.

Spoon batter into greased muffin pans, filling two-thirds full. Bake at 400° for 25 minutes or until golden brown. Yield: about 1½ dozen.

All dressed up for a breakfast of good hot muffins.

Collection of Business Americana

A tray of French Breakfast Puffs (left) and Blueberry Muffins.

FRENCH BREAKFAST PUFFS

⅓ cup shortening
½ cup sugar
1 egg
1½ cups sifted all-purpose
  flour
1½ teaspoons baking powder
½ teaspoon salt
¼ teaspoon ground nutmeg
½ cup milk
½ cup sugar
1 teaspoon ground cinnamon
¼ cup plus 2 tablespoons
  butter or margarine, melted

Cream shortening; gradually add ½ cup sugar, beating until light and fluffy. Add egg, and mix well.

Sift together flour, baking powder, salt, and nutmeg; add to creamed mixture alternately with milk, beginning and ending with dry ingredients.

Spoon batter into greased muffin pans, filling two-thirds full. Bake at 350° for 25 minutes or until lightly browned.

Combine ½ cup sugar and cinnamon; stir well. Remove muffins from pans while still warm; roll each in melted butter, and then in sugar-cinnamon mixture. Cool. Yield: about 1 dozen.

BLUEBERRY MUFFINS

¾ cup fresh blueberries
1½ cups plus 2 tablespoons
  all-purpose flour, divided
2 teaspoons baking powder
¼ cup plus 2 tablespoons
  sugar
½ teaspoon salt
¾ cup milk
1 egg
⅓ cup butter or margarine,
  melted

Dredge blueberries in 2 tablespoons flour, tossing lightly to coat well; set aside.

Combine remaining flour, baking powder, sugar, and salt in a medium mixing bowl. Beat together milk, egg, and butter; add to dry ingredients, stirring until dry ingredients are moistened. Fold in blueberries.

Spoon batter into greased muffin pans, filling two-thirds full. Bake at 400° for 20 minutes or until golden brown. Remove from pan immediately. Yield: about 1 dozen.

Note: Fresh huckleberries may be substituted for the fresh blueberries.

RICHMOND CORN MUFFINS

1 (17-ounce) can whole kernel
  corn, well-drained
½ cup milk
2 eggs, beaten
2 teaspoons sugar
¾ cup all-purpose flour
2 teaspoons baking powder
⅛ teaspoon salt

Combine corn, milk, eggs, and sugar; beat well. Combine flour, baking powder, and salt; stir into corn mixture.

Spoon batter into greased muffin pans, filling two-thirds full. Bake at 350° for 20 to 25 minutes. Yield: 1 dozen.

DATE-BACON MUFFINS

¼ cup butter or margarine,
  softened
2 tablespoons sugar
1 egg
2 cups all-purpose flour
1 tablespoon baking
  powder
½ teaspoon salt
1 cup milk
¾ cup chopped dates
4 slices bacon, cooked and
  crumbled

Cream butter; gradually add sugar, beating well. Add egg; beat until blended.

Combine flour, baking powder, and salt; add to creamed mixture alternately with milk, beginning and ending with flour mixture. Stir in dates and crumbled bacon.

Spoon batter into greased muffin pans, filling two-thirds full. Bake at 400° for 20 minutes. Yield: 1½ dozen.

MOLASSES MUFFINS

2 cups sifted all-purpose flour
1 teaspoon baking powder
½ teaspoon baking soda
½ teaspoon salt
1 egg
½ cup buttermilk
½ cup molasses
2 tablespoons butter or
  margarine, melted

Sift together flour, baking powder, soda, and salt in a medium mixing bowl; make a well in center of mixture. Add egg, buttermilk, molasses, and butter; stir just until dry ingredients are moistened.

Heat well-greased muffin pans in a 400° oven for 3 minutes or until very hot. Spoon batter into hot muffin pans, filling two-thirds full. Bake at 400° for 25 minutes or until golden brown. Yield: 1 dozen.

EXCELSIOR HOUSE ORANGE BLOSSOM MUFFINS

2 cups all-purpose flour
1 tablespoon plus 1 teaspoon
  baking powder
¼ cup sugar
1 teaspoon salt
1 egg, beaten
½ cup orange juice
½ cup orange marmalade
2 tablespoons vegetable oil
½ cup chopped pecans

Combine dry ingredients; make a well in center of mixture. Add egg, orange juice, marmalade, and oil; stir just until dry ingredients are moistened. Fold in pecans.

Spoon batter into greased muffin pans, filling two-thirds full. Bake at 400° for 15 minutes or until lightly browned. Yield: about 1 dozen.

Making orange muffins in the 1920s.

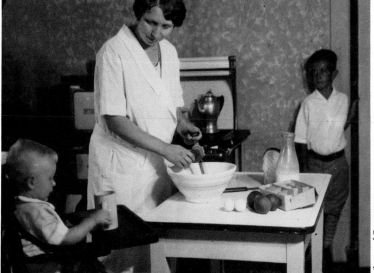

Old Salem Tavern must not be missed by visitors to Winston-Salem. The mealtime action is in any of six dining rooms on two floors of the renovated annex built in 1816. Or one may prefer to eat on the back porch or under the arbor. To walk across honest wooden floors to polished wood tables is to go back in time to the early 1800s. The museum kitchen in the basement reflects the standards of Old Salem's Moravian settlers, justly known for their bread-baking.

Courtesy of Old Salem, Inc.

Original kitchen of the Old Salem Tavern, built in 1784.

RAISIN BRAN MUFFINS

1 cup raisins
¾ cup plus 1 tablespoon all-purpose flour, divided
¾ cup wheat bran
2 teaspoons baking powder
¼ teaspoon baking soda
½ cup sugar
½ teaspoon salt
1 egg, beaten
¾ cup buttermilk
¾ to 1 cup chopped pecans

Combine raisins and 1 tablespoon flour; stir well, and set aside.

Sift together ¾ cup flour, bran, baking powder, soda, sugar, and salt in a large mixing bowl. Combine egg and buttermilk; add to dry ingredients, stirring just until moistened. Stir in dredged raisins and pecans.

Spoon batter into greased muffin pans, filling half full. Bake at 400° for 17 minutes or until golden brown. Yield: about 1½ dozen.

Old Salem Pumpkin Muffins (rear) and Spiced Fruit Muffins.

SPICED FRUIT MUFFINS

½ cup chopped pecans
½ cup chopped raisins
½ cup chopped dates
1¾ cups all-purpose flour, divided
½ cup shortening
1 cup firmly packed brown sugar
2 eggs, beaten
1 tablespoon baking powder
½ teaspoon salt
½ teaspoon ground cinnamon
¼ teaspoon ground nutmeg
½ cup milk

Combine pecans, raisins, dates, and ¼ cup flour; stir well, and set aside.

Cream shortening; gradually add sugar, beating well. Add eggs; beat well. Sift together remaining flour, baking powder, salt, and spices. Add dry ingredients to creamed mixture alternately with milk, beginning and ending with dry ingredients. Stir in dredged pecans, raisins, and dates.

Spoon batter into greased muffin pans, filling two-thirds full. Bake at 400° for 20 minutes or until golden brown. Yield: about 1½ dozen.

OLD SALEM PUMPKIN MUFFINS

⅓ cup raisins
1 tablespoon all-purpose flour
⅓ cup butter or margarine, softened
¾ cup firmly packed brown sugar
1 cup canned pumpkin
½ cup milk
¼ cup molasses
2 eggs, beaten
2 cups sifted all-purpose flour
2 teaspoons baking powder
½ teaspoon salt
½ teaspoon ground ginger
½ teaspoon ground nutmeg
⅛ teaspoon ground cloves

Combine raisins and 1 tablespoon flour; stir well, and set aside.

Cream butter; gradually add sugar, beating well. Add pumpkin, milk, molasses, and eggs, beating well.

Sift together flour, baking powder, salt, and spices; add to creamed mixture, stirring just until dry ingredients are moistened. Stir in raisins.

Spoon batter into greased muffin pans, filling full. Bake at 375° for 20 minutes. Yield: about 1½ dozen.

The Greenbrier graciously presides in White Sulphur Springs, 1857.

GREENBRIER PUMPKIN MUFFINS

½ cup butter or margarine, softened
1 cup sugar
2 eggs
1 cup mashed pumpkin
2 cups all-purpose flour, divided
2 teaspoons baking powder
¼ teaspoon salt
1 teaspoon ground cinnamon
¼ teaspoon ground nutmeg
1 cup milk
½ cup chopped pecans
½ cup raisins

Cream butter; gradually add sugar, beating well. Add eggs, one at a time, beating well after each addition. Add pumpkin, beating well.

Combine 1¾ cups flour, baking powder, salt, and spices; mix well. Add flour mixture to creamed mixture alternately with milk, beginning and ending with flour mixture. Beat well after each addition. Dredge pecans and raisins in remaining flour; fold into batter.

Spoon batter into well-greased muffin pans, filling two-thirds full. Bake at 400° for 25 minutes or until golden brown. Yield: 1½ dozen.

When you awake with a craving for a few days of pampering, head for West Virginia and The Greenbrier, that Southern resort by which others are measured. The palace of ease sits on 6500 wooded acres in White Sulphur Springs; for jewels she wears Mobil's Five Stars and Triple A's Five Diamonds. Exercise such as golf, tennis, swimming, riding, or skeet (or trap) shooting can make you hungry. Good! You cannot have a food fantasy that the chefs at The Greenbrier cannot fulfill; Lucullan feasts are their forte.

SQUASH MUFFINS

½ cup butter or margarine, softened
¾ cup firmly packed brown sugar
¼ cup molasses
1 egg, beaten
1 cup cooked, mashed squash
1¾ cup all-purpose flour
1 teaspoon baking soda
¼ teaspoon salt
¼ cup chopped pecans

Combine butter, sugar, and molasses, beating well. Add egg; beat well. Stir in squash. Combine flour, soda, and salt; add to squash mixture, mixing well. Stir in pecans.

Spoon batter into greased muffin pans, filling two-thirds full. Bake at 375° for 20 minutes. Yield: about 1½ dozen.

OLD-SOUTH COFFEE CAKE

½ cup butter or margarine
1 cup sugar
3 eggs
1½ cups all-purpose flour
2 teaspoons baking powder
½ cup milk
Dash nutmeg
Topping (recipe follows)

Cream butter; gradually add sugar, beating well. Add eggs, one at a time, beating well after each addition.

Sift together flour and baking powder; add to creamed mixture alternately with milk, beginning and ending with flour mixture. Stir in nutmeg.

Spoon mixture into a well-greased and floured 8½- x 4½- x 3-inch loafpan; sprinkle with topping. Bake at 350° for 45 minutes. Let cool in pan 10 minutes; remove from pan. Yield: 1 loaf.

Topping:

¼ cup sugar
¼ teaspoon ground cinnamon
⅛ teaspoon ground nutmeg
2 tablespoons butter or margarine, softened
½ cup chopped pecans

Combine sugar and spices; cut in butter until mixture resembles coarse meal. Stir in pecans. Yield: about ½ cup.

COFFEE CAKE WITH CRUMB TOPPING

1 teaspoon baking soda
1 cup buttermilk
2 cups sifted all-purpose flour
1½ cups firmly packed brown sugar
½ teaspoon ground cinnamon
¼ teaspoon salt
¼ cup plus 2 tablespoons shortening
¼ cup sifted powdered sugar

Dissolve soda in buttermilk; stir well, and set aside.

Combine flour, brown sugar, cinnamon, and salt; stir well. Cut in shortening with a pastry blender until mixture resembles coarse meal. Reserve ¼ cup plus 2 tablespoons flour mixture for topping.

Make a well in center of remaining flour mixture. Add buttermilk mixture; stir until dry ingredients are moistened.

Spoon batter into a greased 8-inch square baking pan; sprinkle reserved flour mixture over batter. Bake at 400° for 35 minutes or until a wooden pick inserted in center comes out clean. Cool in pan 10 minutes. Sprinkle with powdered sugar, and cut into squares. Yield: 9 servings.

Many advertising cards c.1900 featured children.

Serve Sophie's Coffee Cake warm.

GLAZED CINNAMON RING

1¾ cups sugar, divided
2 tablespoons ground cinnamon
¼ cup plus 2 tablespoons shortening
3 eggs
3 cups sifted all-purpose flour
1½ teaspoons baking powder
¾ teaspoon baking soda
¾ teaspoon salt
1½ cups buttermilk
1½ teaspoons vanilla extract
1½ cups sifted powdered sugar
3 tablespoons milk

Combine ¼ cup sugar and cinnamon; mix well, and set aside.

Cream shortening; gradually add 1½ cups sugar, beating well. Add eggs, one at a time, beating well after each addition.

Sift together flour, baking powder, soda, and salt. Add to creamed mixture alternately with buttermilk, beginning and ending with flour mixture. Stir in vanilla. Mix well.

Pour half of batter into a greased 10-inch Bundt pan. Sprinkle three-fourths of reserved sugar-cinnamon mixture over batter in pan. Spoon remaining batter into pan and sprinkle with remaining sugar-cinnamon mixture.

Bake at 350° for 50 minutes or until a wooden pick inserted in center comes out clean. Cool in pan 20 minutes. Remove from pan, and transfer to wire rack. Combine powdered sugar and milk, stirring well; drizzle over cooled cake. Yield: one 10-inch coffee cake.

SOPHIE'S COFFEE CAKE

2 cups all-purpose flour
2 teaspoons baking powder
½ cup plus 2 tablespoons sugar
1 teaspoon salt
1 egg, beaten
¾ cup milk
½ cup butter or margarine, melted
1½ teaspoons all-purpose flour
¼ cup firmly packed brown sugar
1½ teaspoons ground cinnamon
1½ tablespoons butter or margarine, softened
3 tablespoons chopped pecans

Combine 2 cups flour, baking powder, ½ cup plus 2 tablespoons sugar, and salt; stir well. Add egg, milk, and melted butter; beat at medium speed of electric mixer 2 minutes. Pour batter into a greased 9-inch pieplate, and set aside.

Combine 1½ teaspoons flour, brown sugar, and cinnamon; stir well. Cut in butter with a pastry blender until mixture resembles coarse meal. Stir in pecans. Sprinkle mixture over batter in pieplate. Bake at 400° for 30 minutes or until a wooden pick inserted in center comes out clean. Yield: one 9-inch coffee cake.

BISHOPS' BREAD

1 teaspoon baking soda
¾ cup buttermilk
2½ cups all-purpose flour
1½ cups firmly packed brown
   sugar
½ teaspoon salt
½ cup shortening
1 teaspoon baking powder
1 teaspoon ground cinnamon
2 eggs, beaten

Dissolve soda in buttermilk; stir well, and set aside.

Combine flour, sugar, and salt; stir well. Cut in shortening with a pastry blender until mixture resembles coarse meal. Reserve ¾ cup flour mixture for topping.

Add baking powder, cinnamon, buttermilk mixture, and eggs to remaining flour mixture; stir well.

Pour batter into a well-greased 9-inch square pan. Sprinkle reserved flour mixture over batter, and press into batter. Bake at 350° for 30 minutes or until a wooden pick inserted in center comes out clean. Yield: 12 servings.

APPLE STRUDEL

½ cup milk, scalded
1 tablespoon plus 2
   teaspoons butter or
   margarine
1 egg yolk
1 tablespoon sugar
1½ cups sifted all-purpose
   flour
3 medium apples, peeled,
   cored, and thinly sliced
¼ cup sugar
½ teaspoon ground
   cinnamon
½ cup firmly packed
   brown sugar
½ cup drained and chopped
   maraschino cherries
½ cup flaked coconut
½ cup finely chopped
   pecans
¼ cup butter or margarine,
   melted and divided
1 tablespoon milk

Combine milk and 1 tablespoon plus 2 teaspoons butter; stir until butter melts. Set aside to cool.

Combine egg yolk and 1 tablespoon sugar in a large mixing bowl; stir well. Add cooled milk mixture and flour to egg mixture, stirring well.

Turn dough out onto a floured surface, and knead 2 minutes. Cover dough with a warm bowl, and let rest 30 minutes. Roll and stretch dough into a rectangle as thin as possible without tearing.

Place sliced apples evenly over dough, leaving a 1-inch margin around the edges. Combine ¼ cup sugar and cinnamon; spoon over apples. Sprinkle brown sugar, cherries, coconut, pecans, and 3 tablespoons melted butter over the apple mixture. Starting with short side, roll up jellyroll fashion, turning edges under. Pinch seam together to seal.

Place roll in a well-greased 13- x 9- x 2-inch baking pan, and brush top with remaining 1 tablespoon melted butter. Bake at 350° for 45 minutes; brush top with 1 tablespoon milk, and bake 5 minutes or until lightly browned. Remove from pan immediately, and cool on a wire rack. Yield: 1 loaf.

Advertisement for a pecan grower, Baconton, Georgia.

BETTER THAN "STORE-BOUGHT"

When a Southerner thinks of staging a good time for his friends and relatives, his mind turns quickly in several directions at once: What time of day? Mealtime or between-meals snack? With what sort of beverage? Eventually, the mental wheels come to rest like a row of bars on a "one-armed bandit."

Which brings us to the small treats we bake or fry. These are small foods, mind you, not large foods cut-up. And we trot them out as proof that it is often the little things that count. With practice, a cook departs from a basic recipe and develops trademarks for which he or she becomes noted. A Kentucky woman makes drop doughnuts similar to the one in this chapter, for example, but uses a judiciously heavy hand with the nutmeg grater. When a guest wonders why they're better than the usual run of drop doughnuts, he gets a smile of innocent surprise.

Many fried specialties are at their peak of perfection at the exact moment they're fished from the cooking oil, *tout chaud*. We think of calas with that term, but it serves as well for beignets of New Orleans French Market fame. First we inhale the powdered sugar, sneeze slightly, then inhale the beignet, not noticing the seared lips until later.

Now about these terms: We have talked of beignets, which is the French word for fritter. At this point we move on to fritters, the English term for the French *friture*, which means frying, or something fried, or even the grease for frying. It is best not to dwell too heavily on cooking terms; sometimes they can be confusing. We make fritters of rice, nearly any fruit, corn, and other vegetables. One of historic interest is the Arlington Fritter, which will instantly be perceived as having to do with General Robert E. Lee.

Contrary to the preconceived notion of non-residents, Southerners do not fry everything they eat. Teatime, snacktime, or cocktail time, we can bring out little baked things for every hour of the day. While the sun may have set on most of the British Empire, may it never cease to shine on the good English scones and crumpets. From homemade soda crackers to cheese straws, from rusk to (yes) Fat Rascals, we can bake when the spirit moves us.

On stove, Molasses Doughnuts (left) and French Market Beignets (right). On table, Pirogi (rear), Non de Scripts (left), and Fat Rascals (right). Coffee can't be far away.

Morning Call, the French Market, New Orleans, c.1910.

Louisiana State Museum

FRENCH MARKET BEIGNETS

1 package dry yeast
½ cup warm water (105°
   to 115°)
1 cup evaporated milk
1 egg, beaten
¼ cup sugar
1 teaspoon salt
3 cups sifted all-purpose flour
Vegetable oil
Sifted powdered sugar

Dissolve yeast in warm water in a large mixing bowl, stirring well; let stand 5 minutes or until bubbly. Add milk, egg, ¼ cup sugar, and salt; beat well. Gradually blend in flour, mixing well. Cover with a damp cloth, and refrigerate overnight.

Turn dough out onto a heavily floured surface; roll to ¼-inch thickness. Cut into 2½-inch squares; let rest 10 minutes.

Heat 3 to 4 inches of oil to 375°; drop in 3 to 4 beignets at a time. Cook 1 minute or until golden brown on one side; turn and cook other side. Drain on paper towels; sprinkle with powdered sugar. Serve hot. Yield: about 2½ dozen.

DOUGHNUTS— A YANKEE CAKE

6 cups sifted all-purpose
   flour
1 cup firmly packed brown
   sugar
1 package dry yeast
¼ cup warm water (105° to
   115°)
1 cup milk, scalded
2 eggs, beaten
1 teaspoon salt
1 teaspoon ground cinnamon
½ cup butter or margarine,
   softened
Vegetable oil
½ cup sifted powdered sugar

Combine flour and brown sugar; stir well, and set aside.

Dissolve yeast in water, stirring well; let stand 5 minutes.

Combine next 4 ingredients in a large bowl; mix well. Cool to lukewarm (105° to 115°). Add dissolved yeast; mix well. Gradually stir in enough flour mixture to make a soft dough.

Place dough in a greased bowl, turning to grease top. Cover and let rise in a warm place (85°), free from drafts, 1 hour or until doubled in bulk.

Punch dough down; turn out onto a lightly floured surface, and let rest 5 minutes. Knead butter into dough, 2 tablespoons at a time. Roll dough to ½-inch thickness; cut with a 1½-inch biscuit cutter. Place doughnuts on greased baking sheets. Cover and repeat rising procedure 1 hour or until doubled in bulk.

Drop doughnuts, a few at a time, into hot oil (340°). Fry until golden brown, turning once. Drain; sprinkle with powdered sugar. Yield: 4½ dozen.

DOUGHNUT TWISTS

1 small red potato,
  peeled
½ package dry yeast
2 tablespoons warm water
  (105° to 115°)
¼ cup sugar
3 tablespoons shortening
¾ teaspoon salt
¼ cup milk, scalded
3 cups all-purpose flour,
  divided
1 egg, beaten
Vegetable oil
Butter or margarine
Maple syrup

Cook potato in boiling water to cover 15 to 20 minutes or until tender. Drain, reserving ½ cup cooking liquid. Mash potato well, reserving ¼ cup.

Dissolve yeast in warm water, stirring well; let stand 5 minutes or until bubbly.

Combine sugar, shortening, and salt in a large mixing bowl; pour scalded milk and reserved potato liquid over mixture, stirring until shortening is melted. Cool mixture to lukewarm (105° to 115°).

Add ½ cup flour and yeast mixture; stir well. Add 1¼ cups flour, stirring until smooth. Stir in mashed potato, egg, and enough remaining flour to make a soft dough.

Turn dough out onto a floured surface; cover and let rest 10 minutes. Knead dough 5 minutes or until smooth and elastic. Place in a greased bowl, turning to grease top. Cover and let rise in a warm place (85°), free from drafts, 1 hour or until doubled in bulk. Punch dough down; cover and repeat rising procedure 45 minutes.

Punch dough down; turn out onto a lightly floured surface. Cover and let rest 10 minutes. Shape dough into ¾-inch balls; divide balls in half, and roll each half into a 3-inch rope.

Drop shaped doughnut sticks, a few at a time, into deep hot oil (365°). Fry until golden brown, turning once. Drain well on paper towels. Serve hot with butter and maple syrup. Yield: about 7 dozen.

SOPAIPILLAS

1 package dry yeast
1 tablespoon sugar, divided
1½ cups warm water (105° to
  115°)
1 tablespoon shortening,
  melted
1 teaspoon baking powder
1 teaspoon salt
4 cups all-purpose flour,
  divided
Vegetable oil
Honey

Dissolve yeast and 1 teaspoon sugar in warm water in a large bowl, stirring well; let stand 5 minutes or until bubbly. Add remaining sugar, shortening, baking powder, salt, and 2 cups flour; beat at low speed of electric mixer until smooth. Stir in enough remaining flour to make a soft dough.

Place dough in a greased bowl, turning to grease top. Cover and let rise in a warm place (85°), free from drafts, 1 hour or until doubled in bulk.

Punch dough down; turn out onto a lightly floured surface, and let rest 5 minutes. Knead 4 to 5 times. Roll dough to ¼-inch thickness; cut into 3-inch squares. Cut each square in half to form a triangle.

Gently drop dough triangles into deep hot oil (375°); fry only a few at a time, turning once. Cook until sopaipillas are golden brown. Drain on paper towels. Serve hot with honey. Yield: about 3 dozen.

With honey or powdered sugar, Sopaipillas are a treat.

CAKE DOUGHNUTS

2 tablespoons shortening,
  softened
1 cup sugar
2 eggs
1 cup buttermilk
4 cups sifted all-purpose flour
1 teaspoon baking soda
1 teaspoon salt
½ teaspoon ground nutmeg
¼ teaspoon ground cinnamon
Vegetable oil
Sifted powdered sugar

Cream shortening; gradually add sugar, beating well. Add eggs and buttermilk; beat well.

Sift together flour, soda, salt, and spices; add to creamed mixture, beating well. Cover and refrigerate at least 1 hour.

Divide dough in half. Working with one portion at a time, place dough on a heavily floured surface; roll to ¼-inch thickness. Cut dough with a floured doughnut cutter.

Heat 3 to 4 inches of oil to 375°; drop in 3 or 4 doughnuts at a time. Cook 1 minute or until golden brown on one side; turn and cook other side. Drain on paper towels; sprinkle with powdered sugar. Repeat cutting and frying procedures with remaining dough. Yield: about 1½ dozen.

MOLASSES DOUGHNUTS

1 egg, beaten
½ cup sugar
1 cup molasses
½ cup buttermilk
2 tablespoons butter or
  margarine, melted
5 cups sifted all-purpose flour
1 tablespoon plus 2
  teaspoons baking powder
¾ teaspoon baking soda
1 teaspoon salt
1 teaspoon ground nutmeg
1 teaspoon ground cinnamon
1 teaspoon ground ginger
Vegetable oil
1 cup sugar (optional)
2 teaspoons ground
  cinnamon (optional)

Combine egg and sugar in a large mixing bowl; beat well. Add molasses, buttermilk, and butter; mix well.

Sift together flour, baking powder, soda, salt, and spices. Add to molasses mixture, blending well. Cover dough, and chill at least 1 hour.

Divide dough in half. Working with one portion at a time, place dough on a floured surface; roll to ¼-inch thickness. Cut dough with a floured doughnut cutter.

Heat 3 to 4 inches of oil to 375°; drop in 3 or 4 doughnuts at a time. Cook 1 minute or until golden brown; turn and cook other side. Drain on paper towels. Repeat cutting and frying procedures with remaining dough.

Combine sugar and cinnamon; stir well. Roll doughnuts in cinnamon mixture until coated, if desired. Yield: about 2½ dozen.

ORANGE DOUGHNUTS

2 eggs
½ cup sugar
2 tablespoons grated orange
  rind
½ cup orange juice
¼ cup vegetable oil
2½ cups all-purpose flour
2 teaspoons baking powder
1 teaspoon salt
Vegetable oil
Sifted powdered sugar

Beat eggs 2 minutes at medium speed of electric mixer; add sugar, beating well. Add rind, juice, and oil; mix well.

Combine flour, baking powder, and salt; add to egg mixture, beating until smooth.

Drop batter by level tablespoonfuls into deep oil heated to 375°. Fry until golden, turning once. Drain well on paper towels. Roll each doughnut in powdered sugar. Yield: about 2½ dozen.

"Dough Nuts—A Yankee Cake," from *The Virginia Housewife*, goes like this: "Dry half a pound of good brown sugar; pound it and mix it with two pounds of flour, and sift it; add two spoonsful of yeast, and as much new milk as will make it like bread: when well risen, knead in half a pound of butter, make it in cakes the size of half a dollar, and fry them a light brown in boiling lard."

Yankee cakes or not, the South took out the adoption papers so long ago that we regard them as family: Yeast doughnuts, cake doughnuts, and all the variations are included here, even the holes. Our recipes are somewhat more detailed now, making it easy for anyone to have homemade, not "store-bought," doughnuts.

THE LADY.

Oh, see the nice Lady.

She seems to be Well-Fed, Well-Bred and Well-Read.

How Daintily she goes about her work. Oh, she is Frying Doughnuts.

Yes. She uses Cottolene for Shortening and also to Fry them in, so it is Dainty work and the Result is Airy, Puffy Doughnuts.

Not Greasy and Heavy like the Ones Mother used to make.

But where are the Doughnuts?

Well, you see, they were so Good, she ate them up as Fast as she Fried them.

Oh, what will her Hungry Husband Say?

He will Laugh, and Say:

"Out of the Frying Pan into the Fryer."

POTATO DOUGHNUTS

3 tablespoons shortening
¾ cup sugar
3 eggs
1 cup cooked, mashed
  potatoes
4¼ cups all-purpose flour
1 tablespoon plus 1 teaspoon
  baking powder
1 teaspoon salt
1 teaspoon ground mace
⅛ teaspoon ground
  nutmeg
½ cup milk
Vegetable oil
Sifted powdered sugar

Cream shortening; gradually add sugar, beating well. Add eggs, one at a time, beating well after each addition. Add mashed potatoes; beat well.

Sift together flour, baking powder, salt, and spices; add to creamed mixture alternately with milk, beginning and ending with flour mixture. Chill dough at least 1 hour.

Turn dough out onto a heavily floured surface; roll to ⅓-inch thickness. Cut dough with a floured doughnut cutter.

Heat 3 to 4 inches of oil to 375°; drop in 3 or 4 doughnuts at a time. Cook 1 minute or until golden brown on one side; turn and cook other side. Drain on paper towels. Sprinkle with powdered sugar. Yield: 3 dozen.

Baskets of Doughnut Holes (front) and *Potato Doughnuts.*

DOUGHNUT HOLES

1½ cups all-purpose flour
2½ teaspoons baking powder
⅓ cup sugar
½ teaspoon salt
½ cup milk
1 egg, beaten
1 tablespoon butter or
  margarine, melted
Vegetable oil
½ cup sugar
1 teaspoon ground cinnamon

Sift together flour, baking powder, ⅓ cup sugar, and salt. Add milk, egg, and butter; mix with a wooden spoon until smooth.

Drop batter by teaspoonfuls into deep oil heated to 375°. Fry until golden brown, turning once. Drain well.

Combine ½ cup sugar and cinnamon; stir well. Roll doughnuts in cinnamon mixture until coated. Serve warm. Yield: about 3½ dozen.

BISCUIT PUFFS

½ teaspoon baking soda
¾ cup buttermilk
2 cups sifted all-purpose flour
½ teaspoon salt
¼ cup plus 1 tablespoon
  shortening
Vegetable oil
Honey (optional)

Dissolve soda in buttermilk; stir well. Combine flour and salt; cut in shortening until mixture resembles coarse meal. Sprinkle buttermilk mixture evenly over flour mixture, stirring until dry ingredients are moistened. Turn dough out onto a lightly floured surface; knead lightly 4 to 5 times.

Roll dough to ⅛-inch thickness; cut into 2-inch squares. Deep fry in hot oil (350°) until golden brown. Drain on paper towels; serve immediately with honey, if desired. Yield: 2 dozen.

Calas merchant selling rice fritters. Painting by Léon Frémaux.

ARLINGTON FRITTERS

1 package dry yeast
¼ cup warm water (105° to 115°)
1¾ cups milk
2 tablespoons butter or margarine
3 tablespoons sugar
1 teaspoon salt
4 cups all-purpose flour, divided
1 egg, beaten
Vegetable oil
Hot maple syrup

Dissolve yeast in warm water, stirring well; let stand 5 minues or until bubbly.

Scald milk; add butter, sugar, and salt, stirring until butter melts. Let cool to lukewarm (105° to 115°).

Gradually add 2 cups flour, beating well. Stir in dissolved yeast and egg. Add remaining flour; beat well. Cover and let rise in a warm place (85°), free from drafts, 1 hour or until light and bubbly.

Gently drop mixture by tablespoonfuls into deep hot oil (375°). Cook 1 minute or until golden brown on one side; turn and cook other side. Drain on paper towels. Serve hot with syrup. Yield: 2 dozen.

CALAS "TOUT" CHAUD

2 eggs, separated
1 cup sugar
1 cup cooked rice
2 cups all-purpose flour
2 teaspoons baking powder
Vegetable oil
Sifted powdered sugar

Beat egg yolks; gradually add sugar, beating well. Add rice, flour, and baking powder, stirring well.

Beat egg whites (at room temperature) until stiff peaks form; gently fold into rice mixture just until the dry ingredients are moistened.

Drop mixture by tablespoonfuls into deep hot oil (375°); cook 1 minute or until golden brown. Turn and cook other side. Drain well. Sprinkle with powdered sugar. Serve hot. Yield: about 1½ dozen.

NON DE SCRIPTS

1¼ cups all-purpose flour
3 tablespoons sugar
⅛ teaspoon salt
3 egg yolks, beaten
¼ cup plus 1 tablespoon milk
Vegetable oil
⅓ cup sifted powdered sugar

Combine flour, sugar, and salt. Add egg yolks and milk; stir until dough leaves sides of bowl.

Turn dough out onto a lightly floured surface; knead 10 to 12 times or until smooth. Roll dough to ⅛-inch thickness; cut into 3-inch squares. Fold each square in half, and make 4 slashes on the side parallel to the folded edge.

Carefully drop each pastry square into deep hot oil (370°); cook only a few at a time. Fry until golden brown. Drain well. Sprinkle with powdered sugar. Yield: about 1½ dozen.

The original recipe for Arlington Fritters appeared in *The Virginia Housewife*, published in 1824 by Mary Randolph, a kinswoman of General Robert E. Lee. It later appeared in a 1907 cookbook where it was credited to Mary Tabb Lee, daughter-in-law of the General.

After mixing the dough, so goes the original, "Make into balls the size of a walnut and fry a light brown in boiling lard. Serve with wine and sugar and molasses."

CORN FRITTERS

1½ cups all-purpose flour
2 teaspoons baking powder
1 teaspoon salt
½ teaspoon pepper
½ cup milk
2 cups whole kernel corn
2 eggs, beaten
2 tablespoons butter or
   margarine, melted
1 tablespoon finely chopped
   onion

Sift together flour, baking powder, salt, and pepper in a large bowl.

Combine milk, corn, eggs, butter, and onion; mix well, and stir into dry ingredients.

Drop mixture by tablespoonfuls into deep hot oil (375°). Fry until golden brown, turning once. Drain on paper towels. Serve hot. Yield: about 1 dozen.

SMITH HOUSE PUMPKIN FRITTERS

5 eggs
1½ cups sugar
3 cups bread flour
2 teaspoons baking powder
½ teaspoon salt
1¼ teaspoons ground
   cinnamon
¼ teaspoon ground nutmeg
1 (16-ounce) can pumpkin
2 tablespoons plus 2
   teaspoons vanilla extract
Butter or margarine, melted

Beat eggs in a large bowl; add sugar, mixing well.

Combine flour, baking powder, salt, cinnamon, and nutmeg; mix well. Add to egg mixture, beating well. Stir in pumpkin and vanilla.

Drop mixture by tablespoonfuls into hot butter; cook over medium heat until golden brown, turning once. Drain on paper towels. Yield: about 7½ dozen.

Fresh fruit is the basis for Apple Fritters (rear) and Fruit Fritters.

APPLE FRITTERS

2 eggs, separated
1 cup milk
1 tablespoon brandy
2 cups all-purpose flour
3 cooking apples, peeled,
   cored, and thinly sliced
Butter or margarine, melted
Sifted powdered sugar

Beat egg yolks until thick and lemon colored. Add milk and brandy, beating well. Beat egg whites (at room temperature) until stiff peaks form; gently fold into flour.

Dip apple slices in batter. Fry in hot butter until golden brown and tender, turning once. Sprinkle with powdered sugar. Yield: about 3 dozen.

FRUIT FRITTERS

1¼ cups all-purpose flour
2 teaspoons baking powder
Dash of salt
1 cup milk
2 eggs
3 pears, peeled, cored, and
   thinly sliced
Vegetable oil
Sifted powdered sugar

Combine flour, baking powder, salt, milk, and eggs; mix well. Dip pear slices in batter.

Carefully drop pear slices into deep hot oil (375°); cook only a few at a time. Fry until fritters are golden brown, turning once. Drain on paper towels. Sprinkle with powdered sugar, and serve hot. Yield: about 3 dozen.

RICE FRITTERS

1½ cups sifted all-purpose
   flour
1½ teaspoons baking powder
½ teaspoon salt
1 cup cooked rice, cooled
1 egg, beaten
⅔ cup milk
Vegetable oil
Maple syrup

Sift together flour, baking powder, and salt in a medium mixing bowl. Stir in rice. Add egg and milk; stir well.

Drop batter by tablespoonfuls into deep hot oil (375°). Cook 1 minute or until golden brown on one side; turn and cook other side. Drain on paper towels. Serve hot with maple syrup. Yield: 1½ dozen.

Corn comes in many colors, including blue or green; the word is the same in some Indian dialects. When blue corn is ground into masa harina (corn flour), it is preferred by many in the Southwest for tortillas, despite its off-putting gray color. Modern milling has replaced the *metate* once used by the Indians and Mexicans for grinding. And most of our tortillas are factory-made. It takes great dexterity to form them by hand. We roll ours.

CORN TORTILLAS

2 cups yellow cornmeal
½ cup plus 2 tablespoons
   all-purpose flour
1 teaspoon salt
1¼ cups hot water

Combine cornmeal, flour, and salt; stir well. Gradually stir in water, mixing well.

Shape dough into 1½-inch balls, and place on a lightly floured surface. Roll each ball into a very thin circle about 6 inches in diameter.

Heat a lightly greased griddle over medium heat; cook tortillas 2 minutes on each side or until lightly browned. Yield: about 1 dozen.

FLOUR TORTILLAS

3 cups all-purpose flour
½ teaspoon baking powder
1 teaspoon salt
1 tablespoon shortening
1 cup hot water
Melted butter or margarine
   (optional)

Combine flour, baking powder, and salt; stir well. Cut in shortening with a pastry blender until mixture resembles coarse meal. Gradually stir in water, mixing well.

Shape dough into ½-inch balls, and place on a lightly floured surface. Roll each ball into a very thin circle about 4 inches in diameter.

Heat an ungreased cast-iron griddle over medium heat; cook tortillas 2 minutes on each side or until lightly browned. Pat tortillas lightly with spatula while browning the second side if they puff during cooking. Serve hot with butter, if desired. Yield: about 3½ dozen.

Note: Tortillas may also be cooked in an ungreased electric skillet heated to 375°.

Again, the daily bread: Mexican girl prepares tortillas while several bake on stove at rear. Robstown, Texas, 1939.

Maryland Moonshine Crackers: Marvelous with cheese.

MARYLAND MOONSHINE CRACKERS

1 egg
¼ cup milk
2 tablespoons lard, melted
2 tablespoons butter or
  margarine, melted
2 cups all-purpose flour
½ teaspoon baking powder
½ teaspoon salt
1 egg white
2 tablespoons sesame
  seeds

Beat egg until light and frothy. Add milk, lard, and butter; beat well.

Combine flour, baking powder, and salt in a medium mixing bowl; stir well. Gradually add egg mixture, beating well. Chill dough at least 2 hours.

Roll dough to ⅛-inch thickness; cut with a 1½-inch biscuit cutter. Place on ungreased baking sheets. Brush tops with egg white, and sprinkle with sesame seeds. Bake at 400° for 10 to 12 minutes. Yield: about 5½ dozen.

CROUTONS

12 slices bread
¼ cup butter or margarine,
  softened

Spread bread slices evenly with butter. Trim crust; cut bread into ½-inch cubes. Place on baking sheet in a single layer. Bake at 375° for 10 minutes or until browned. Yield: about 3 cups.

SIPPETS

9 slices bread

Remove crusts from bread. Cut each slice into 5 strips. Place on a lightly greased baking sheet. Bake at 450° for 5 minutes or until lightly toasted. Serve with soup or oysters. Yield: about 4 dozen.

HOMEMADE SODA CRACKERS

4 cups all-purpose flour,
  sifted
1 teaspoon salt
3 tablespoons butter or
  margarine
½ teaspoon baking soda
2 cups milk

Combine flour and salt in a large mixing bowl; cut in butter until mixture resembles coarse meal. Dissolve soda in milk; add to flour mixture, stirring well.

Turn dough out onto a floured surface. Pound dough with a wooden mallet or rolling pin for 30 minutes or until surface is covered with air bubbles, folding dough over frequently.

Roll dough to ⅛-inch thickness, and cut into 2-inch squares. Place on well-greased baking sheets in even rows, and prick tops of squares with tines of fork. Bake at 375° for 20 minutes or until lightly browned. Yield: about 7 dozen.

MR. PACA'S RUSK

1 cup milk, scalded
3 tablespoons sugar
2 tablespoons butter or
  margarine
1 teaspoon salt
1 teaspoon sugar
1 package dry yeast
¼ cup warm water (105° to
  115°)
3 eggs, beaten
4 to 5 cups all-purpose flour,
  divided

Combine milk, 3 tablespoons sugar, butter, and salt in a large bowl; stir until butter melts. Cool to lukewarm (105° to 115°).

Dissolve 1 teaspoon sugar and yeast in warm water, stirring well; let stand 5 minutes or until bubbly.

Combine yeast and milk mixtures and eggs, stirring well. Gradually add 2 cups flour, mixing well. Cover and let rise in a warm place (85°), free from drafts, 1 hour or until doubled in bulk. Stir in enough remaining flour to make a stiff dough.

Turn dough out onto a lightly floured surface; knead 10 minutes or until smooth and elastic. Place dough in a greased bowl, turning to grease top. Cover and repeat rising procedure 1 hour. Punch dough down, and turn out onto a lightly floured surface. Cover; let rest 10 minutes.

Divide dough into 5 equal portions, shaping each into a smooth ball. Place on greased baking sheets; press down lightly with fingertips until dough resembles a bun.

Cover and repeat rising procedure 45 minutes or until doubled in bulk. Bake at 325° for 25 minutes or until lightly browned. Cool on wire racks. Yield: 5 rusks.

Note: Rusks may be used whole as buns; or, for a crisper rusk, each may be cut in ½-inch thick slices and baked at 275° for 40 minutes.

There has always been a need in our menus for a little something to go with soup, oysters, and cheese. We know, as did generations before us, the value of crisp, dry crumbs for thickening, extending, breading. Sippets are slices of bread cut into sticks and dried out in the oven, then served as a crunchy accompaniment. They are a time-honored way of using up last week's bread before the current week's baking takes place.

Rusk is an interesting little side trip the baker takes. We who have bought dry, crisp rusks may not have realized that rusks (plural) start out as rusk (singular), which is a delicious yeast bread loaf.

It was prized along the Eastern Seaboard in both forms. Mary Randolph says in *The Virginia Housewife*, that the yeast dough should be made "softer than bread. Make it at night. In the morning, if well risen, work in six ounces of butter, and bake it in small rolls; when cold, slice it, lay it on tin sheets, and dry it in the oven." Apparently she did not enjoy it fresh from the oven, but cooled and sliced it immediately and put it back in the oven to dry.

The revised 1811 recipe we use here, however, first bakes rusk into loaves the size of large hamburger buns, which are split, buttered, and served freshly toasted. When stale, rusk may be cut into halves and dried out in the oven to become rusks, with an "s."

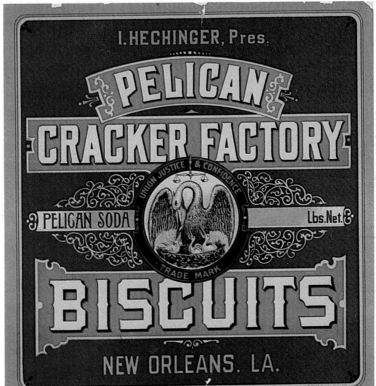

Biscuit can label, Pelican Cracker Factory, early 1900s.

TEA SCONES

2 cups pastry flour
1 tablespoon plus 1 teaspoon baking powder
¼ cup sugar, divided
½ teaspoon salt
3 tablespoons butter or margarine, softened
1 egg, beaten
½ cup plus 1 tablespoon milk
2 tablespoons butter or margarine, melted

Sift together flour, baking powder, 2 tablespoons sugar, and salt in a medium mixing bowl. Cut in 3 tablespoons butter with a pastry blender until mixture resembles coarse meal.

Combine egg and milk; add to flour mixture, stirring until well blended.

Turn dough out onto a floured surface; knead 3 to 4 times. Roll dough to ¼-inch thickness, and cut with a 2-inch biscuit cutter. Place scones in lightly greased muffin pans. Brush scones with melted butter, and sprinkle evenly with remaining sugar. Bake at 400° for 15 minutes or until lightly browned. Yield: about 2½ dozen.

CRUMPETS

2 cups milk, scalded
1 egg, beaten
3 cups all-purpose flour
1 teaspoon salt
1 package dry yeast
¼ cup warm water (105° to 115°)
¼ cup butter or margarine, melted
Butter or margarine (optional)
Strawberry jam (optional)

Cool milk to lukewarm (105° to 115°) in a medium mixing bowl; add egg, beating well. Gradually stir in flour and salt, beating well.

Dissolve yeast in warm water, stirring well; let stand 5 minutes or until bubbly. Stir in ¼ cup butter. Add yeast mixture to flour mixture, beating well. Cover and let rise in a warm place (85°), free from drafts, 1 hour or until doubled in bulk.

Grease 4-inch muffin rings, and place on a hot, lightly greased griddle. Pour batter into muffin rings, filling two-thirds full. Reduce heat to low, and cook crumpets 8 to 10 minutes on each side. Remove from rings; set aside to cool. Repeat procedure with remaining batter. Split crumpets and lightly toast. Serve with butter and strawberry jam, if desired. Yield: 10 crumpets.

Henry Morrison Flagler at tea with friends, Palm Beach, 1895.

The Henry Morrison Flagler Museum

Cozy setting for tea epitomizes Southern charm. Tea Scones (front) and Crumpets are in the English tradition. Crumpet is from Old English "crump," for curled, bent.

SCOTCH SODA SCONES

4 cups all-purpose flour
2 teaspoons cream of tartar
1 teaspoon baking soda
1 teaspoon salt
¼ cup shortening
1¼ cups buttermilk
1 egg, beaten
2 teaspoons maple syrup

Combine flour, cream of tartar, soda, and salt; stir well. Cut in shortening until mixture resembles coarse meal.

Combine buttermilk, egg, and syrup; stir into flour mixture just until dry ingredients are moistened.

Turn dough out onto a lightly floured surface. Divide dough into 8 equal portions, shaping each into a smooth ball. Press down with fingertips to ½-inch thickness. Cut into 4 equal pie-shaped pieces. Prick each with the tines of a fork. Place on greased and floured baking sheets. Bake at 400° for 10 to 12 minutes. Yield: about 3 dozen.

EASY GRAHAM SQUARES

1 cup shortening
1 cup sugar
2 eggs
1 teaspoon baking soda
1 cup milk
5 cups all-purpose flour
½ teaspoon baking powder
½ teaspoon salt

Cream shortening; gradually add sugar, beating until light and fluffy. Add eggs, one at a time, beating well after each addition.

Dissolve soda in milk. Combine flour, baking powder, and salt; add to creamed mixture alternately with milk mixture, beginning and ending with flour mixture.

Divide dough into 3 equal portions. Place on ungreased baking sheets. Roll dough into ¼-inch thick 10- x 12-inch rectangles. Bake at 400° for 10 minutes or until browned. Cut into 2-inch squares while still warm. Yield: 7½ dozen.

FAT RASCALS

4 cups all-purpose flour
1 tablespoon baking powder
1 tablespoon plus 1 teaspoon sugar
1½ cups butter or margarine, softened
1¼ cups milk
1 cup currants
Butter or margarine, melted

Combine flour, baking powder, and sugar; reserve ¼ cup for dredging currants. Add butter and milk to remaining flour mixture, stirring until blended.

Dredge currants in reserved flour mixture; stir into dough.

Turn dough out onto a floured surface; roll to ½-inch thickness. Cut dough into rounds with a 1¾-inch cookie cutter. Place on greased baking sheets. Bake at 400° for 15 minutes or until lightly browned. Yield: about 4 dozen.

Mother's little helpers promote vegetable shortening in nineteenth-century advertisement.

COOKING AND EATING BOTH A DELIGHT, WITH **ARMOUR'S** CELEBRATED ILLINOIS CREAMERY **BUTTERINE.**

B. HARRIS & SONS, LITH. PHILA.

For porch or patio: Frosty beer with Caraway Salt Sticks.

CARAWAY SALT STICKS

1 package dry yeast
½ cup sugar, divided
2 cups warm water (105° to 115°)
3 tablespoons shortening, melted
1 egg, beaten
2 tablespoons plus 1 teaspoon salt, divided
6½ cups all-purpose flour, divided
1 egg, beaten
2 tablespoons caraway seeds

Dissolve yeast and 1 teaspoon sugar in warm water in a large bowl, stirring well. Let stand 5 minutes or until bubbly. Add remaining sugar, shortening, 1 egg, 1 teaspoon salt, and 3½ cups flour; beat at low speed of electric mixer until smooth. Stir in enough remaining flour to make a soft dough.

Place dough in a greased bowl, turning to grease top. Cover and let rise 1 hour or until doubled in bulk. Punch dough down, and let rest 5 minutes.

Turn dough out onto a lightly floured surface, and knead 4 to 5 times. Divide dough into 4 equal portions. Divide each portion into 10 pieces. Roll each piece into an 8-inch rope, and place on greased baking sheets. Brush top of breadsticks with beaten egg. Sprinkle with remaining salt and caraway seeds.

Cover and repeat rising procedure 50 minutes or until doubled in bulk. Bake at 425° for 10 minutes or until golden brown. Place on wire racks to cool. Yield: 40 sticks.

Parmesan Salt Sticks:

Substitute ¼ cup grated Parmesan cheese for the caraway seeds. Continue with recipe as directed.

Garlic Salt Sticks:

Substitute 2½ tablespoons garlic salt for the caraway seeds and 2 remaining tablespoons salt. Continue with recipe as directed.

CHEESE PUFFS

1 cup (4 ounces) shredded
   sharp Cheddar cheese
½ cup butter or margarine,
   softened
1 cup all-purpose flour
24 pecan halves
Sifted powdered sugar

Combine cheese and butter;
mix well. Add flour, mixing well.
Chill at least 1 hour.

Roll dough to ½-inch thickness; cut with a 1½-inch biscuit
cutter. Place on ungreased baking sheets. Top each with a
pecan half. Bake at 450° for 10
minutes or until lightly
browned. Place on wire racks to
cool. Sprinkle with powdered
sugar. Yield: about 2 dozen.

Cheese Straws (front) and
Cheese Puffs (rear):
Whenever savory is needed
as counterpoint to sweet.

CHEESE STRAWS

1 cup all-purpose flour, sifted
½ teaspoon baking powder
1 cup (4 ounces) shredded
   sharp Cheddar cheese
½ cup butter or margarine
3 tablespoons cold water

Combine flour and baking
powder. Cut in cheese and butter with a pastry blender until
mixture resembles coarse meal.
Sprinkle water evenly over flour
mixture; stir with a fork until
ingredients are moistened.
Shape into a ball.

Use a cookie press to shape
dough into 2½-inch long strips,
following manufacturer's in-
structions, or roll dough to ⅛-
inch thickness on a lightly
floured surface, and cut into
2½- x ½-inch strips.

Place strips on ungreased
baking sheets. Bake at 400° for
12 minutes or until crisp. Place
on wire racks to cool. Yield:
about 5 dozen.

PIROGI

1 (12-ounce) carton
   small-curd cottage
   cheese
1 tablespoon butter or
   margarine, melted
1 egg, beaten
2 cups all-purpose flour
⅓ cup water
½ teaspoon salt
2 eggs
12 cups boiling water
1 tablespoon salt
Melted butter or margarine
   (optional)

Combine cottage cheese, 1 tablespoon butter, and 1 beaten
egg; stir well, and set aside.

Combine flour, water, and ½
teaspoon salt in a medium bowl;
add 2 eggs, stirring well.

Turn dough out onto a floured
surface, and divide into 8 equal
portions; roll each portion into a
ball. Roll each ball into a 4-inch
square. Place 1 tablespoon
cheese mixture in center of each
square. Moisten edges with
water; fold over to form a triangle. Press edges together with
fork tines to seal.

Place turnovers, a few at a
time, in boiling water with 1 tablespoon salt. Cook 12 minutes,
stirring occasionally to prevent
turnovers from sticking to bottom of pan. Drain on paper
towels; serve with melted butter, if desired. Yield: 8 servings
or 16 appetizer servings.

Hot, savory turnovers:
every cuisine has one,
from the steamed
dumplings of China to the
empanadas of Mexico. Crust
may be raised or flat, the filling anything from cabbage
to cheese. Pirogi is the larger
version; piroshki the
smaller. When you've sealed
in the filling, you can decide
whether to boil or fry them,
or brush them with butter
and bake.

ACKNOWLEDGMENTS

Adobe Oven Bread adapted from *Melting Pot* by The Institute of Texan Cultures, University of Texas at San Antonio. By permission of The University of Texas Institute of Texan Cultures, San Antonio, Texas.

Alabama Corn Griddle Cakes courtesy of Mrs. Ruth Spitzer, Mobile, Alabama.

Amish Cakes, Caraway Salt Sticks, Crumpets, Generals, Maryland Beaten Biscuits, Maryland Fried Mush, Maryland Moonshine Crackers, Mr. Paca's Rusk, Popovers, Scratch Backs adapted from *Maryland's Way* by Mrs. Lewis R. Andrews and Mrs. J. Reaney Kelly. By permission of The Hammond-Harwood House Association, Annapolis, Maryland.

Anna Maude's Honey Almond Rolls courtesy of The Anna Maude Cafeteria, Oklahoma City, Oklahoma.

Arkansas Cornmeal Flapjacks, Cassie's Egg Cornbread, Mrs. Yohe's Original Brown Rice Bread, Swiss Egg Braid adapted from *Prairie Harvest* by St. Peter's Episcopal Church Women. By permission of St. Peter's Episcopal Church Women, Hazen, Arkansas.

Arlington Fritters, Doughnuts-A Yankee Cake adapted from *Virginia Cookery, Past and Present* by The Women's Auxiliary of Olivet Episcopal Church, Franconia, Virginia.

Baking Powder Bread courtesy of Burrus Milling, Saginaw, Texas.

Benne Seed Biscuits adapted from *Charleston Receipts*, collected by The Junior League of Charleston, ©1950. By permission of The Junior League of Charleston, South Carolina.

Boca Raton Pecan Rolls courtesy of The Boca Raton Hotel and Club, Boca Raton, Florida.

Boone Tavern Hush Puppies, Florida Orange Biscuits, Florida Orange Bread, French Breakfast Puffs, Sweet Orange Roll-Ups adapted from *The Gasparilla Cookbook* by The Junior League of Tampa, ©1961. By permission of The Junior League of Tampa, Florida.

Bread Brake Biscuits, Irish Bread courtesy of Mrs. Caroline Lavender, Birmingham, Alabama.

Cake Doughnuts courtesy of Mrs. Delilah Averhart, Fultondale, Alabama.

Casselman Inn Applesauce Nut Bread courtesy of The Casselman, Grantsville, Maryland.

Cathead Biscuits courtesy of The Kitchen of Arlington Antebellum Home and Gardens, Birmingham, Alabama.

Corn Fritters, Potato Ice Box Rolls adapted from *Favorite Recipes of the Red River Valley*, collected by The Gleaners Class, First Methodist Church, Shreveport, Louisiana. By permission of The Gleaners.

Cornmeal Batty Cakes adapted from *Grace Hartley's Southern Cookbook*, collected from *The Atlanta Journal*, Atlanta, Georgia, ©1976 by Grace Hartley. By permission of Doubleday & Co., Inc.

Cornish Saffron Bread adapted from *The Southern Cookbook* by Marion Brown, ©1951. By permission of The University of North Carolina Press, Chapel Hill, North Carolina.

Corrie Hill's Banana Nut Bread, Chicken Biscuits, Whole Wheat Honey Bread, adapted from *Out of Kentucky Kitchens* by Marion Flexner, ©1949. By permission of Franklin Watts, Inc., New York.

Cross Creek Hush Puppies, Miniature Luncheon Muffins adapted from *Cross Creek Cookery* by Marjorie Kinnan Rawlings, ©1942. By permission of Charles Scribner's Sons, New York.

Doughnut Sticks adapted from *Caprock Girl Scouts Cookbook*, ©1975. By permission of the Caprock Girl Scouts, Lubbock, Texas.

Excelsior House Orange Blossom Muffins courtesy of Excelsior House, Jefferson, Texas.

Fat Rascals, Scotch Soda Scones adapted from *The Monticello Cook Book* by the University of Virginia Hospital Circle, Richmond, Virginia, published 1941.

Fruit Drop Biscuits, Johns Island Cornbread adapted from *The South Carolina Cookbook* by the South Carolina Homemakers Council, Columbia, South Carolina, ©1953. By permission of The University of South Carolina Press, Columbia, South Carolina.

Glazed Cinnamon Ring adapted from *Welcome Back to Pleasant Hill* by Elizabeth C. Kremer. By permission of Shakertown at Pleasant Hill, Harrodsburg, Kentucky.

Graham Bread by Mrs. Francis D. Stallworth, Sr., Beatrice, Alabama, first appeared in *Stallworth Roots and Recipes*.

Greenbrier Pumpkin Muffins courtesy of The Greenbrier, White Sulphur Springs, West Virginia.

Grove Park Inn Bran Muffins courtesy of The Grove Park Inn and Country Club, Asheville, North Carolina.

Hermann-Grima Brioche, New Orleans French Bread, Round Crusty Loaf from the collection of The Hermann-Grima Historic House, New Orleans, Louisiana.

Herren's Sweet Rolls courtesy of Herren's Restaurant, Atlanta, Georgia.

Hotel Roanoke Spoonbread courtesy of Hotel Roanoke, Roanoke, Virginia.

Johnny Cakes, Peanut Biscuits adapted from *Plantation Recipes* by Lessie Bowers, ©1959. By permission of Robert Speller & Sons, New York.

Kentucky Beaten Biscuits adapted from *Famous Kentucky Recipes*, compiled by the Cabbage Patch Circle, Louisville, Kentucky, ©1952. By permisison of the Cabbage Patch Circle.

Lemon Bread, Squash Muffins courtesy of Shakertown at Pleasant Hill, Harrodsburg, Kentucky.

Louisiana Bullfrogs adapted from *The Picayune Creole Cookbook*, published 1936.

Mock Crackling Bread with Creole Celery Sauce by Mrs. McCormick Gondran, New Orleans, Louisiana. Courtesy of Mrs. Gondran's family.

Neiman-Marcus Monkey Bread adapted from *Neiman-Marcus, A Taste of the Past.* By permission of Neiman-Marcus, Dallas, Texas.

Oklahoma Cornmeal Rolls courtesy of Mrs. Sally Gray, Admore, Oklahoma.

Old Salem Pumpkin Muffins courtesy of Old Salem Tavern, Winston-Salem, North Carolina.

1935 Chocolate Bread adapted from *Forgotten Recipes*, compiled and updated by Jaine Rodack. By permission of Wimmer Brothers Books, Memphis, Tennessee.

Pirogi by Dr. and Mrs. Lewis A. Stallworth, East Lyme, Connecticut, first appeared in *Stallworth Roots and Recipes.*

Prize-Winning Coffee Cake adapted from *State Fair of Texas Prize-Winning Recipes.* By permission of State Fair of Texas, Dallas, Texas.

Salzburger Raisin Bread courtesy of Mrs. JoAnne Morgan Conaway, Springfield, Georgia.

Shaker Daily Loaf, Shaker Friendship Bread, Shaker Salt-Rising Bread adapted from *We Make You Kindly Welcome* by Elizabeth C. Kremer. Published by Shakertown Pleasant Hill Press, ©1970. By permission of Shakertown at Pleasant Hill, Harrodsburg, Kentucky.

Shirley Graham Muffins adapted from *Famous Colonial Recipes* by Maude Bomberger, published 1906.

Smith House Pumpkin Fritters courtesy of Smith House, Dahlonega, Georgia.

Southern Kitchen's Cinnamon Rolls courtesy of Southern Kitchen, Dallas, Texas. John and Dorothy Sohrweide, owners.

Stagecoach Inn Hush Puppies courtesy of Stagecoach Inn, Salado, Texas.

Sunflower Seed Bread by Mr. Clarke J. Stallworth, Birmingham, Alabama, first appeared in *Stallworth Roots and Recipes.*

Swedish Rye Bread adapted from *From Norse Kitchens* by Our Savior's Luthern Church Women, Clifton, Texas. By permission of Our Savior's Luthern Church Women.

Tennessee Crackling Bread courtesy of Mr. James Deery Eakin, Jr., Shelbyville, Tennessee.

The Peabody's Vanilla Muffins courtesy of The Peabody Hotel, Memphis, Tennessee.

Virginia Corn Pones adapted from *Recipes from Old Virginia* by The Virginia Federation of Home Demonstration Clubs.

Whipping Cream Biscuits adapted from *Bayou Cookbook* by Thomas J. Holmes, Jr., ©1969. By permission of St. Mary's Printers, Franklin, Louisiana.

Winkler Honey Wheat Bread courtesy of Winkler Bakery, Old Salem, North Carolina.

The Universal Family Dough Mixer !

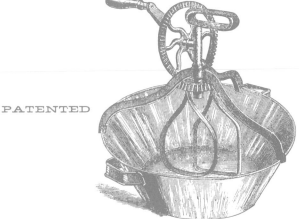

PATENTED   JULY 23, '78.

INDEX

·THE·WOMAN·WHO·WILL·READ·